I Speak for Lebanon

Kamal Joumblatt

Translated by Michael Pallis

As recorded by Philippe Lapousterle

Zed Press, 57 Caledonian Road, London N1 9DN

I Speak for Lebanon was first published in French by
(Editions) Stock, 14 Rue de l'Ancienne Comedie, 75006
Paris; and in English by Zed Press, 57 Caledonian Road,
London N1 9DN in 1982

Translation Copyright © Zed Press, 1982

Typeset by Margaret Cole
Copyedited by Anna Gourlay
Proofread by R. Howe and Anna Gourlay
Cover photo by Catherine Leroy
Cover Design by Jacque Solomons
Printed by Redwood Burn, Trowbridge, Wiltshire

British Library Cataloguing in Publication Data

Joumblatt, Kamal
  I speak for Lebanon.
  1. Lebanon — Politics and government
  I. Title   II. Pour le Lisban. *English*
  956.92'044   DS87

  ISBN 0-86232-097-6

U.S. Distributor
Lawrence Hill and Co., 520 Riverside Avenue, Westport,
Conn. 06880, U.S.A.

Contents

Publisher's Note

Kamal Joumblatt

The Joumblatts, one of the two most prominent Druze families in the Lebanon, have been a force in the area's political life for centuries. Kamal Joumblatt continued that tradition. Born on December 6, 1917 at Moukhtara, the family's stronghold in the mountains behind Beirut, he studied law and philosophy at the Sorbonne and then at the Jesuit University in Beirut. In 1946, he was elected to the Chamber of Deputies. A few years later, he founded the Progressive Socialist Party, which brought together many of the more left-wing Deputies and adopted a firm anti-imperialist stance. Shortly afterwards, Joumblatt put his socialist principles into practice by distributing large tracts of his family's lands to poor peasant farmers.

During the uprising of 1958, Joumblatt and his followers sided with the Arab nationalists and seized control of the important Chouf Region. The revolt was eventually put down, but it did succeed in forcing a compromise solution and in undermining Lebanon's inequitable, confessionalist political system.

In subsequent governments, Joumblatt was successively Minister of Education, Minister of Public Works and Minister of Justice, in which capacity he legalized the Communist Party, which had been banned for the previous 25 years. He also actively sought an agreement with the representatives of the hundreds of thousands of Palestinian refugees encamped in the Lebanon.

By 1975, he had become the major figure on the Left in the country. As leader of the Lebanese National Movement, he played a central role in the Civil War, and strongly opposed the Syrian invasion which ensued.

Kamal Joumblatt was both rebel and statesman, mystic and politician. His sincerity, commitment and dedication to the Lebanese idea were beyond doubt. On March 16, 1977, shortly after completing the initial manuscript for this book, he was brutally murdered. With his death the Arab world has lost one of its truly great figures.

Philippe Lapousterle

Philippe Lapousterle is a journalist who has lived in Lebanon since the beginning of the Civil War. He is the Beirut correspondent of the French national daily, *Le Matin,* and of Radio Monte Carlo. From Beirut, he also publishes a quarterly information bulletin for specialists in the area, *Carnets du Monde Arabe.*

This book is the fruit of a great many hours Lapousterle spent working with Kamal Joumblatt in the latter's home at Moukhtara and in his campaign headquarters. The Lebanese leader annotated every page of the final transcript just before his death.

Preface

Throughout the West, it is reasonably easy to depict a particular politician: a few characteristic and oft-repeated themes, certain particular attitudes, membership of this or that party, a heavy but reasonably coherent timetable, and you have him. But with Kamal Joumblatt it did not work that way. There was always more to discover: infinite complexity, innumerable facets, a sense of time quite specific to the region. Above all, each of his ideas was constantly being linked to the practical and the concrete. When a person dispenses justice, when one is a military leader, a skilful parliamentarian, a maker and breaker of governments, a feudal chieftain, a religious authority and a progressive Third World militant, when one has discovered one's inner light thanks to a guru, when, having been brought up on Latin and Greek culture, one's daily experience is of the infinite complexities which make up the reality of the Arab world today, and especially when the most deep-rooted tradition which surrounds one insists that both stranger and friend are above all one's 'brothers', then one finds that everything becomes familiar and no problem remains a total mystery.

The West will doubtless long remain an indispensable purveyor of administrators and technocrats, but it may be that we will shortly have to turn to the East if we are to find real statesmen. Kamal Joumblatt exemplified certain qualities; those who knew him will not forget it.

On 16 March 1977, when this text had only just been finished, Kamal Joumblatt was assassinated. The Lebanese leader had carefully read each of these pages: they were all annotated in his own hand. His disappearance, and then certain technical obstacles, have delayed the publication of what has now become his political testament. This long delay was, in the end, good for something; by sheltering the book from the distorting glare of publicity, it made it possible to preserve its spirit. Had it been published soon after the socialist leader's brutal murder, each clan and each camp would have seized upon certain selected lines chosen at random to prove their own case, or to lose themselves in purely conjectural criticisms.

Although the war raged on throughout the writing of this book, it remains primarily a testimony and a reflection. Kamal Joumblatt analyses the facts, illustrates the mechanisms, describes people and develops a philosophy. He alone amongst the actors in the Lebanese war can do so with any lucidity and

1

without parochialism; his deep roots in Lebanon and his uncontested Arabicity spared him the fear of persecution, the biased narrow-mindedness which usually characterizes the chiefs of a minority.

In May 1976, during our first conversations, Kamal Joumblatt was doing battle, militarily and politically, against a growing number of enemies. Just before he died, the Lebanese leader had stood back somewhat. A fragile truce had been imposed on his country by the arrival of the Arab League troops. But as everybody knew, none of the problems had been solved for all that; in fact everything, from Arab dissensions and international rivalries to Israeli strategy, indicated that Lebanon would remain the privileged battle-ground for future conflicts in the Middle East.

Fratricidal war was once again going to soak this small country in blood. Kamal Joumblatt intended to stand aside when it happened, as he had always done whenever irrationality and illogic were allowed to rule the roost. 'I do not know whether it is still possible to engage in political activity in Lebanon anymore,' he told me. 'I will probably concentrate on more interesting subjects for a while. We will have to wait for things to settle down. At the moment, every policy leads to confrontation, everything is slipping from our grasp.'

It was not long before his prophecy was realized. At present, Lebanon still faces the same problems. Fourteen armed contingents from as many different nations are encamped here, and thousands more Lebanese have fallen in battle since Kamal Joumblatt's death.

Those who knew the old Lebanon constantly evoke the country's delight-ful climate, the proverbial hospitality of the Levantines and the merits of Lebanese tolerance, which made it possible for 17 different communities to live in peace together. Lebanon was once offered as an example of harmony. 'The land of milk and honey' said the tourist brochures; 'a haven for exiles and a crossroad of civilizations' said the intellectuals. 'The necessary channel for all the Arab world's gold' added the bankers.

After having suffered a multiplicity of invasions, Lebanon lived for a long time under the aegis of the Ottoman Empire, which granted a substantial level of autonomy to Mount Lebanon. At the end of the First World War, Mount Lebanon, along with two other provinces, was put under French Mandate by the League of Nations. In 1926, Greater Lebanon endowed itself with a Constiution, and in 1943 the famous National Pack was agreed, an 'unwritten' pact which regulates the difficult equilibrium between the country's denominations to this day.

Beirut soon became the hub of the Arab world, largely thanks to the particular aptitude for trade of the Lebanese. Lebanon was careful not to participate in any of the four Israeli-Arab wars, but the facts of geography meant that it could not avoid the consequences of those conflicts. The country became the unwilling host of more than 300,000 Palestinians, whose presence as an armed force was seen as a threat by a significant section of the population and their leaders.

On 13 April 1975, a Palestinian bus on its way through a Christian quarter was caught in a hail of bullets, under circumstances which are still not clear: 27 Palestinians died. This was the starting point for a pitiless war; in less than two years there were over 30,000 dead and twice as many wounded. Syria, a powerful neighbour, could not remain indifferent, and intervened to restore the balance, at first helping the Progressive/Palestinian camp, then saving the Christians from a defeat which seemed inevitable.

Following the October 1976 Arab Summits of Riyadh and Cairo, the Syrian troops traded their battle fatigues for the uniform of the Arab League's troops.

Kamal Joumblatt, the uncontested military and political leader of the coalition between the Lebanese left and the Palestinian resistance was killed soon after Lebanon's very relative pacification.

In this region of the world where passion plays as much a part in politics as does reason, the *Moallem* will remain the man who stood for compromise and balance, for the compromise between ideals and the practical. 'Yet he fought,' some may object. Indeed he did, just as one day it may be necessary to fight in order to impose an overall compromise in the Middle East. For rationality is not the basis of politics in the Middle East. Passion, fear, mistrust, the struggle for survival, extremism and dreams, the resort to arms; these are the rulers here, and the enemies of compromise and reasoned agreement. The Middle East is the region of the 'historical non-compromise'.

But perhaps one day the peoples of the Levant, tired of increasingly bloody wars, will manage to make themselves heard. A consensus will emerge and the rulers will have to accept it. Reason, true compromise and the spirit of Kamal Joumblatt will have finally triumphed.

Philippe Lapousterle

1. The Plot

'Implements for killing people in the Third World are the most lucrative of all commodities . . .'

The plot against Lebanon was first hatched in 1967. The Egyptians and Syrians having lost the war, the isolationists, as we call the ultra-Maronites, felt that the time had come to reassert themselves and push for a Lebanese Lebanon separate from the Arab world. A meeting was organized, to which intellectuals, monks, Maronite League representatives, politicians, personalities, ex-Presidents of the Shamun Republic and their entourage, deputies and journalists were all invited. The aim of the meeting was to analyse the events of 1967 and their consequences, in order to work out a new plan of action that would take into account the fact that Israel had emerged as the most powerful State in this area of the Middle East. The defeat reduced the risk of any reaction by the Arabs, especially the Syrians, who were known to be hostile to the development of isolationism in Lebanon. Nasser had suffered a defeat which was political as much as military. His image, as the champion of the idea of an Arab nation and the mythical symbol of Arab unity and nationalism, had been tarnished. Nasser as a leader, as demiurge, represented the ideal of struggle for the national and social liberation of the Arab masses who had so long been oppressed, first by the Ottoman occupation and then by British and French colonialism.

The isolationists (Falangists and others) believed that this was their opportunity to disengage from Arab nationalism — which they had accepted only as a compromise or necessary evil during the 1943 struggle for the independence of Lebanon — and to reinforce the specific character of a Lebanon free from all outside obediences. The events of 1841-60 (the Maronite offensive) had been a first step towards this differentiation and autonomy from the Arab-Muslim world. As far as the isolationists were concerned, the two concepts overlapped: an Arab was by definition a Muslim. The Syrians, in particular, were seen as the enemy, whilst Nasserism represented the dynamism of a triumphant Arab nationalism.

The Falangists (the isolationist movement's pro-fascist youth organization) began to arm themselves extensively towards 1969. Our information suggests that during this period leading up to the events of 1975-76, they had between

7,000 and 8,000 trained men under arms and possessed several hundred heavy machine guns, cannons and mortars.

The October 1973 Yom Kippur war gave them pause for thought. Despite a few, limited defeats (slight retreat in the Golan and the Israeli breakthrough in the Deversoir), the main point was that the Arabs had smashed the Israeli Bar-Lev line. The Syrians and the Egyptians had fought well, their morale was good, and the general feeling was that the Arabs had won an important victory, since Israel would clearly have been defeated had it not been for massive American support. Syria, especially, had deployed impressive armed forces, including 2,000 tanks. For those who feared Syrian expansionism and influence in Lebanon, this was more than a little disturbing. The new Syrian-Egyptian alliance forged in the common struggle gave further cause for concern. To these anti-Arab Lebanese, Syria had emerged as a minor 'great power'; the defeat of 1967 was quite forgotten.

The isolationists began to call for preventive steps against the 'Syrian menace', a refrain which was taken up at the time in the columns of the newspaper *Al Nahar*. A new meeting was called, and was attended by that confused and ambivalent, if highly cultured, individual, President Charles Helou. I cannot say why such a civilized man, who claimed to be so broadminded, should have been attracted by this new vigil of arms: perhaps one should always be careful of pure intellectuals. Perhaps he himself had not yet completely internalized and accepted the idea of Arab-Lebanese hybridization. Intellectuals are always quick to take fright, and many Maronite intellectuals were dragged along by this fear, this constantly reiterated false alarm. They ended up as enemies of any national economic and social progress. They buried themselves under a mass of false or distorted concepts about Islam and Arabism and allowed themselves to be swept along by the mainstream.

Those who represented the collective will of the fundamentalist Maronites continued to meet, in an atmosphere of outdated Jesuitism; personalities and public figures gathered in a shadowy and artificial freemasonry, and day by day the plot became more convincing, more incisive. In complete secret, negotiations were opened with Israel, Europe and the Americans. It was decided that since the Arabs had become more powerful, the Lebanese Army would have to be reinforced and supplied with new weapons; enough 'to stand up to a Syrian invasion for a few days', just long enough for American and other Western reinforcements to arrive. All this despite the fact that, in the past, the isolationists had always opposed any increase in the Lebanese Army's troops or arsenal. The U.S., France and the Arab countries were all requested to send arms, under the fallacious pretext that the Lebanese Army had to cope with Israel's incursions and aggression along our southern frontier. Perhaps the Israeli attacks were the result of collusion, perhaps not. The fact is that they were exaggerated out of all proportion by the press, and used to fan nationalist feelings. It is always easy to use Israeli actions in order to create an artificial, popular enthusiasm. All that is required is a little manipulation of public opinion, on the lines of the Dreyfus affair.

The Lebanese State thus asked for help from the Arab States, and was given it. The Lebanese press, possibly the one worthwhile press in the Arab world, had considerable influence in the matter. Another important factor was the naivety, the lack of cynicism, one might even say the stupidity of the Arab political leaders, who have never understood anything about Lebanon, about dualism or about the manoeuvrings of the isolationists. Irrational Arabism, as always, was blinded by its own mythology. Political Islam, so often ill-informedly generous and debonair, let itself be duped. Weapons and ammunition streamed in from Saudi Arabia, from Egypt, from Libya. Gifts from America and purchases from France completed the new arsenal. The supplies continued to arrive right up to the events of 1975[1] were triggered off. During this period, from 1969 to 1975, Sleiman Frangie, ex-President of the Republic, was kept informed about the decisions of the secret conclave, that Kfour before the Kfour, that Kaslik before the Kaslik.[2] Our fate was constantly being determined by the more or less clearly elaborated decisions of this cabal.

Sleiman Frangie knew about these decisions, perhaps he even participated in them, motivated by the same fears as the others. For him as for them, it has to be stressed that the crucial point was to reinforce the Lebanese Army, so that it could withstand the first clash with Syria, could resist for a few days or even a few hours, during which Europe, 'our good friends in France', the United Nations or the United States could respond to appeals for help, as the U.S. had done in 1958 when President Shamun called for support.[3]

At the time, of course, the Syrians had no intention whatsoever of attacking or invading Lebanon, but fear creates so many illusions, and the Syrians could only respond to what was happening in a way that reinforced that fear. It was a vicious circle. Meanwhile the Maronite legions, the Falangists, and Shamun's 'Tigers' were receiving more and more arms. Sleiman Frangie himself, as he has admitted to some of his guests, was encouraging the Maronite factions' armaments bonanza. As he put it: 'I have given the Commanding General of the Army [the neurotic Iskandar Ghanem] the green light to buy weapons and pass them on to the Falangists and their allies.' A substantial proportion of the incoming military equipment was thus secretly handed over to the Falangists, at the Army's expense.

The Israelis had no intention of attacking Lebanon either, despite their long-term territorial ambitions concerning the southern parts of our country. On the contrary (as events were later to show), they saw Lebanon as a twin brother, another segregationist state disguised as a democracy. Hence the historical alliance between the Christian minority in Lebanon and the Jewish minority against the Arab-Muslim world. Close direct and indirect contacts were gradually established between the isolationists and the Israelis. Other discreet contacts were made in the United States, France and Europe, mainly in West Germany, a country which seems to have played an important role in Lebanese affairs, perhaps because of the Catholicism of its leaders. The first sketch of the plot was being filled in.

The Falangists began to set up their training camps throughout the country, with the full knowledge of the authorities; indeed, Army Officers actively participated. Shamun and the other factions, such as President Frangie and his son Tony, followed suit, preparing their men for combat. The vigil of arms was underway! Meanwhile, emissaries — often enough Pierre Gemayel[4] and Camille Shamun themselves — toured the Arab capitals spreading misinformation and calming fears. Each Arab leader was told precisely what he wanted to hear.

The Army purchased the first batch of weapons for the Falangists from Bulgaria, and other contacts with Eastern Bloc countries followed. Since it was important to camouflage the insurrection that was being prepared, the C.I.A., which has ample stocks of weapons and munitions manufactured in the Eastern Bloc, generally provided the rest. According to diplomatic sources in Beirut, some $250 million were allocated to procure the destabilization of Lebanon. The American Administration was apparently determined to sacrifice tens of thousands of Lebanese victims to the Canaanite god Moloch, simply in order to ensure that the U.S. had its way at an eventual Geneva conference. Apart from these generous suppliers, there was also that major international firm, the Mafia, which supplies weapons from almost everywhere (with the possible exception of the Soviet Union) and which is run by an American who sells guns like other people sell hats. His charges are 10 to 15% higher than the official rates but he can supply weapons of every calibre from every country, be it communist or capitalist, European or American. The whole world sells arms through this Mafia-controlled consortium. Implements for killing people in the Third World are the most lucrative of all commodities.

Lebanese emigres also played an active part in broadcasting the necessary propaganda and telling the right lies to the respective Arab leaders in order to pave the way towards the massacre. But they were not alone: even our Syrian friends — Minister Khaddam in particular — were later to pick up the refrain, and talk of 'fighting communism and Soviet influence in Lebanon'. We were made aware of this propaganda only shortly before events exploded, but friends had told us that trouble was brewing. Edmond Rabbath, a well-known advocate of democraticization, constitutional reform and secularization of the State in Lebanon, had warned us that when he was in Switzerland American friends had told him: 'You will shortly witness the destruction of the economic structures and institutions of Lebanon. An international conspiracy is underway.' And indeed, a few months later, once the conflict had broken out, we witnessed the systematic and deliberate destruction — not just of our shops — but of our banks, our factories, and of everything that made up our economic potential. It was like a gale of madness howling through the country.

When the conflict began, a friend, the Ambassador of a major country, told me: 'It will not be over quickly. It will go on for a year and a half, maybe two. The Americans, through the C.I.A., have set aside a special fund of $250 million to provoke and sustain a war in Lebanon. Those dollars will buy guns for the isolationists and finance their war.' I asked him, 'But how can these people get weapons from the Communist countries?' 'Listen,' he said 'the C.I.A. in Europe has stocks of every sort of weapon, Soviet, Bulgarian, Polish, whatever, bought either directly or in advance from the manufacturers, or on the open market, as the need arises. Such weapons are used to provoke trouble in many Asian, African and Latin American countries.' At the time, I was astonished; my interlocutor was after all a serious man who knew what he was talking about. 'The war has various purposes,' he added, 'notably to teach the Palestinians a lesson, to push the Arab world into a hornet's nest and to pave the way to Geneva.' The truce during which this conversation took place soon collapsed and the war continued, more bloody and barbarous than ever. My friend was right. Later, out of curiousity, I asked the American Ambassador if what I had been told was true. 'No, of course not,' he replied. Then I mentioned it to Mr. Dean Brown, President Ford's special envoy to Lebanon. 'The C.I.A.,' I said, 'seems to be behind what is happening in Lebanon. Neither side seems able to put an end to the conflict. An invisible hand seems to be fanning the flames of this war.' Again, I was met with blank denials. 'The U.S. has no communist arms in Europe' I was told. Soon afterwards, the American Embassy even issued a special communique on the subject. Perhaps American diplomats are not supposed to know too much about what their secret services are up to.

Recently, an American Senator of Lebanese descent, James Abu Rizk, a brave and sincere man, challenged the U.S. Administration by effectively declaring that the U.S. was providing arms to the Maronites in Lebanon through Israel. Various American and European newspapers have also raised the issue. It is certainly true that Israel has provided Shamun and the Falangists with weapons and ammunition. Furthermore, before the 1975 events occurred, some Arab countries had themselves sent several truckloads of arms to the other side; even Syria supplied ex-President Frangie. Perhaps they did so quite innocently, in response to a request and in the hope of winning the bellicose President's favour. His son, Tony, also received Syrian weapons, I believe, probably as a gesture of friendship by individuals who owed favours to him and his clique, individuals close to the entourage of President Hafez-el-Assad (President Assad himself is of course a man of un-impeachable integrity). The Falangists also received guns from Jordan (how did these truckloads of weapons manage to cross right through Syria? One day, I will ask President Assad). The Jordanian Army trained many Falan-gists in the use of heavy weapons in Jordanian camps. Shamun too was probably supplied — indirectly — by his friend, King Hussein. Indeed, to be frank, the King of Jordan must have been aware of what was about to take place in Lebanon. Quite naturally, he gave it his blessing — given his antagonism towards the P.L.O. Later, during the struggle itself, we were repeatedly told by friends that the Saika, a pseudo-Palestinian organization, had given guns and especially munitions to the Falangists when they were running short.

Did Iran provide weapons? I cannot say. What I do know is that Mr.

Shamun is a good friend of the Iranians, along with his little mentor, Kazem Khalil. Supposedly, Shamun, his son and his associates, have made a great deal of money in Iran by exporting bananas from Lebanon. Shamun was given a licence and a sort of *de facto* monopoly on the banana trade with Iran. It is also said that Iran subsidized Shamun and other personalities, including a noted Lebanese journalist who frequently visits the country. Those who go often to Teheran usually go cap in hand.

I hope that one day I, too, shall visit Iran, but I certainly do not intend to go as a beggar. I would like to go there to admire the magnificent mosques, the gardens, the pre-Islamic structures and the works of art. The great names of Iranian literature are particularly evocative for me. We have relatives there too, Druses like ourselves (*Dine Makhfi*, the secret religion). The Shah himself is a man of character who has managed to steer an independent course in many areas. Obviously, however, one cannot but reproach him for the persecutions which prevail within his country, especially the system of terror established by SAVAK (the Iranian Cheka) and the bloody repression of the Iranian left. In any case, I do not know to what extent the Iranians have intervened in our affairs in Lebanon; I do not intend to spin fables.

What I do say is that the Americans – and Israel – were deeply involved. Other major European countries stand equally condemned, according to information we have from Shamun and the Falangists; it is said on the other side that West Germany provided them with guns, ammunition and military training. The same is reported of Belgium, another notably pro-Israeli European country. One should never forget what was and still is at stake: the political reduction and encirclement of the P.L.O., with the aim of forcing that organization to go to Geneva and accept a proposed solution to the Israeli-Palestinian conflict.

As part of the Lebanese National Movement,[5] we naturally came to the aid of the Palestinian people. We refused to accept any readymade solutions, as we would refuse clothes cut to fit another man's shoulders. We, therefore, had to be punished, the Palestinians and ourselves, for our impudence. The Americans very skilfully managed things so that Syria would intervene in an area which has always been of interest to her. After all, Syria and Lebanon were one nation before the partition of 1919. The Syrian Ba'athist regime, caught between the hammer of Arab nationalism and the anvil of immediate self-interest, prestige and political security, allowed itself to slip from political arbitration to military intervention. Some surrogate was required after the bitterly resented loss of large parts of the Golan. As the reader will recall, Mr. Kissinger's to-ing and fro-ing never resulted in any steps to effect the restitution of these lost territories to Syria. Finally, there were also the Syrian Ba'athists' long-denied ambitions, their harassing rivalry with the Iraqi Ba'athist regime and their 2,000 tanks that were just waiting for an adventure. Their embarrassment was further accentuated by the fact that Syria had put itself in a false position. Damascus had presented itself as the champion of an uncompromising Arabism, nationalism and 'Palestinianism', against President Sadat's over-hasty and unnecessary steps towards peace in

September 1975 (the Sinai Agreements). The woolliness of both the Egyptian and the Syrian positions, based entirely on the ambiguous Security Council decisions of 1973, the obscurity and lack of specificity (as to content, extent and delineation of frontiers) of the compromise reached concerning the solution to the Palestinian problem, all contributed to rendering the Syrian political offensive ineffective in the long term. An unspecific and vague compromise is always a bad compromise.

A while ago I proposed to President Assad and his colleagues that they take a clear and unambiguous stance for or against a compromise which, after much thought, I personally consider the least offensive and most acceptable to the various tendencies in Arab and Palestinian political thought, namely to demand the implementation of the 1947 U.N. decisions, as a *modus vivendi*. The eventual Palestinian State would thus cover a larger area and 1,200,000 refugees would be able to return to their homes in Israel. The various movements of the Palestinian resistance would agree to such a solution, which was originally put forward by President Habib Bourguiba and, since it would enable the Palestinian refugees to go home, their presence in Lebanon and elsewhere would cease to be a problem. Also, the surface area of the proposed Palestinian State would be much larger, and would include much more good agricultural land than would be the case should Israel withdraw only to its pre-1967 borders. The new state I envisaged would cover 46% of the territory of historical Palestine. In Israel, the Jewish settlers from the Diaspora would gradually become 'resemiticized' through contact with the 1,600,000 Palestinian Arabs who would be living alongside them. With time, peace would come to this part of the world.

President Assad answered that, given present circumstances, it was difficult for him to go along with such a compromise, for all that it was the least inhuman available and the closest to some form of justice. I found in this rejection a further example of that oft manifested tendency of Arab statesmen to prefer vagueness in practice whilst using the language of extremism in theory. In 1947-48, the Arabs lost Palestine and saw a Zionist State established because they proved incapable of agreeing upon a clear and positive attitude, because they failed to understand the international position of the Jewish community after the War, and because they continued to be inconsistent and hostile towards each other, often indulging in intemperate verbalism. In particular, I am thinking of the project of a Judeo-Arab federation proposed as a last recourse by the U.N., and which the Arabs were foolish enough to reject. Again, what a terrible mistake it was for certain Arab countries to call on the Palestinians to leave Palestine — in order to return later by force — instead of massively arming them at the time, thereby enabling them to stay where they were and prevent the Zionization of Palestine.

Our own party, the Lebanese Progressive Socialist Party, was asked to go to war against President Sadat's Egypt. We refused, and merely expressed our objective opinion concerning the Sinai compromise. The P.L.O., also, was subjected to sometimes brutal pressures, insisting that they denounce the pact and break with Egypt. Iraq, along with Algeria, went no further than to condemn the Sinai Agreement. There were no verbal excesses and no break with Egypt.

In the Arab world, as in a windmill, you often have to shout as loudly as possible to make yourself heard, but in practice Saudi Arabia often has the last word in the politics of this Arab Levant. This was manifest at the Riyadh mini-summit and the immediate cessation of the Syrian offensive against our forces at Bhamdun. President Sadat, with his Egyptian sense of humour, made a discreet reference to the fact during the Cairo Arab summit,[6] raising a few smiles all round. The reconciliation (happy or unhappy) is now an accomplished fact; the debate is closed.

I continue to believe that if Saudi Arabia and the rich Arab oil-producing states were to advance Egypt, impoverished and battered as she is by four successive wars, the few billions a year she needs to settle her $11 billion debt and to accelerate her economic development, the situation would change radically, both in terms of the Arab confrontation with Israel and on the international level. There would be a greatly improved chance of reaching the best possible Arab-Palestinian-Israeli compromise. Similarly, the problem of Syria's political ambitions could be resolved by more substantial financial assistance, enabling the regime to cope with the pressures from below. Everybody is 'compressed' in this Arab world of ours. There is room for everybody in the Middle East, but not for every ambition. And there is still far too great a contrast between the poverty of some states and the opulence of others.

Also, we have to settle our problems of co-operation with the U.S.S.R. Why should the Soviets always be obliged to advance us millions of dollars worth of military equipment and economic aid and never get anything in return? The people of the Soviet Union face vast development tasks of their own, in Siberia and even in European Russia.

To reintegrate Lebanon, dissociated from the old Syria in 1919, remains a long-standing dream of certain Syrian political figures. This dream was given a new urgency by the recent political and economic difficulties of the leaders of the Ba'ath Party in Damascus. Indeed, in a moment of frankness, President Assad, defending the Arabism of ex-President Frangie, told Yasser Arafat: 'You are full of reproaches for Sleiman Frangie, but you should know that he is the only Lebanese President who would immediately accept to sign a treaty unifying his country with Syria should I ask him to do so.' Obviously the Frangies, father and son, enjoyed a whole range of relations in Damascus linking them with the multifarious clientele of the Baabdu Palace.[7] The apparently outspoken, rough and slightly caustic temperament of Sleiman Frangie has its attraction, and certainly he was popular in Damascus. Even I would admit that Frangie himself, a man with a certain sense of honour, has never been despicable; what is indubitable is that he has always lacked a good mentor and good advisers.

The Syrian leaders were handicapped externally by the constant harassment of Iraq, Libya, the P.L.O. and the Palestinian opposition, and internally by the mood of a public tired of waiting for some compromise leading to a partial or total withdrawal of Israeli troops from the Golan. They had every reason to be receptive to the project of a Syrian-Jordanian confederation and later, given events in Lebanon, to the idea of a Syrian-Jordanian-Lebanese confederation. The Lebanese Ba'ath Party, which in fact is merely a branch of the one in Damascus, has been suggesting such a scheme for over three years. Only one avenue could lead to such a goal: a *rapprochement* with the Maronites, in which Syria would appear as the real protector of the Lebanese isolationists yet would be able to integrate them within Arabism. The other problem was to contain and restrict the Palestinians, whose independent attitude and success on the international level (over a hundred States have expressed support for their cause) was an embarrassment to everybody, especially to those countries part of whose territory has been under Israeli occupation since 1967. Since the lost territories could not be regained directly, a strategem or detour was sooner or later going to be essential. The heroism displayed during the Ramadan War, and the premature air of triumph which ensued, required some realization of the hopes which had inspired them. Heroic attitudes are difficult to cope with in these dictatorial countries: the myth of greatness is a constant preoccupation of their statesmen. Recrimination against the avarice of the oil-producing countries and their refusal to provide a genuine level of aid were further factors in the development of resentful feelings.

Another element in this mercantile puzzle was King Hussein's constantly reiterated pretension to assume a mandate over the proposed Palestinian principality, to be set up on the West Bank of the Jordan as compensation to those whose homeland had been seized.

The Palestinians were frightening everybody, in that they were not only drawing left-wing tendencies in behind them, but also all the partisans of change in the more decadent Arab States. They had to be controlled. Whether Syria was to provide camouflage for the operation, become a participant, or completely appropriate the exercise of the mandate over the Palestinians, there could be no doubt that she would have to be involved. Kissinger, a German Jew well versed in the Oriental dialectic, in Hegel's philosophy and in political and military strategy, very skilfully seized the opportunity to revive the myth and push for direct action. He actively encouraged the intervention in Lebanon. His telephone call to Rabin, to calm the growing anxieties of Israelis, is now famous.

The prospect of material gain was also a factor. The Saika[8] tore through Beirut like a cyclone, looting everything. Nearly half the Lebanese population imitated them, in an exhibition of moral decadence for which one can only blame the rapid or illicit enrichment of the few in the past, the disorganization of the State and the re-emergence of the 'rapacious Bedouin' in the ranks of the combatants (a phenomenon more common amongst the Christian isolationists, already familiar with liberal materialism, than amongst the patriots and Muslims). The flea market was flooded with goods looted from the houses, villas, banks, shops and seraglios of Beirut. After all, Persian carpets are a good long-term investment . . . . Gangsterism, the ugly face of

Bedouinism, reigned triumphant. But perhaps the pillage was not quite so accidental as one might think. Lebanon had, after all, been an object of envy throughout the Arab world.

Finally, Damascus continued in its efforts to establish some sort of joint political and military command structure with the Palestinians. The latter refused any very close integration, which would have restricted their political independence and reduced their room for manoeuvre. Perhaps it was a good idea, but its execution would have required parity and equality in the negotiations. As all the arms supplies for the Palestinian resistance were coming through Syrian territory, the P.L.O. was, in practice, under considerable pressure. The Saika already constituted a major intervention in what, properly speaking, were purely Palestinian affairs, but it was not enough in the eyes of the Ba'athists of Damascus, who considered and still consider all Palestinians as an integral part of the Syrian people; Palestine is simply 'Southern Syria'. According to Damascus, a closer integration between their forces and the Palestinian revolution would have permitted a general alignment.

There is always a great deal of junk in the bazaar of Oriental politics — I wonder whether politics in Europe are as complicated. For instance, Yasser Arafat was resented for his good relations with Saudi Arabia, a country whose largest subsidies go to the P.L.O. He was also criticized for getting on so well with everybody and for not having become involved in the stupid and factitious quarrels which divide so-called progressive and so-called reactionary Arab regimes. In practice, the words have lost their meaning through overuse; all the leaders of the less privileged Arab States were hungrily attentive to the prospect of oil money coming their way. Tutelage over the Palestinian movement, which more or less everybody lays claim to, would have been used to extract more money from the oil-rich States, who still stubbornly insist upon paying out only the bare minimum needed to prevent the economies of Egypt, Syria and other developing Arab countries from collapsing completely.

The Soviet Union remained in the background, incapable, as we ourselves often were, of understanding this elaborate game, and as disgusted as we were with the dualistic policies of the Arabs, their lack of lucidity and their occasional ability to turn their coats and abandon their best friends. The U.S.S.R.'s policy is still at a stage when she can disengage from her interests in the Middle East. Of course, the Soviets were nervous when the Americans began to assemble the Sixth Fleet off Lebanon and Cyprus, at the very moment when President Assad's troops were penetrating into Lebanese territory to the east, with at most a hundred tanks deployed in a tiny triangle behind the Deir Zenun bridge, two or three kilometres within our frontiers. France, too, had sent a few warships. The Americans were protesting that they did not want Syria to intervene. The Soviets began to move their own squadron into position. There had even been talk of a European intervention to save Lebanon, with France leading the expedition. But neither the Americans nor the Russians would accept such an intervention: the Middle

East was the private hunting ground of the two super-powers. And the Gaullists were no longer in power in France, to countervail this balancing act and provide some genuine political assistance to Lebanon. Giscard and his hesitant technocrats were all too anxious to spare the political interests of the Americans.

I remember a conversation I had at the time with Ambassador Dean Brown, President Ford's special envoy. I had thanked him for the interest the United States was taking in the safeguarding of Lebanon's independence and integrity. I told him of my fears concerning the sudden influx of Syrian troops. It was during the period when the isolationists were being defeated everywhere – in Beirut, in the mountains, at the gates of Kesruan, in the north and in Zahle. 'Oh, they won't come any closer than Deir Zenun, you know,' he answered. He had told an old friend, ex-Prime Minister Abdullah Yafi, the same thing. Hearing him speak, one might have thought the United States was running the entire operation. At the time, we took the Americans to be sincere, but shortly afterwards we learnt of the bargain Kissinger had struck with the Israelis. There was no further mention of a European intervention, or of an American memorandum addressed to Syria: the Syrians had been given the green light to penetrate Lebanon. Kissinger had pulled off his conjuring trick. As far as he was concerned, Israel's interests were paramount and the road to Geneva had to be opened up. The Syrian regime had, therefore, to be granted a prestige victory to ensure its participation in future peace negotiations. As usual, we were the dupes and the victims of the great powers involved in this 'eastern question'.

The Israelis were vexed and then anxious about the Syrian intervention, but Kissinger's phone call to Rabin explained everything to their satisfaction: 'But don't you understand? Just let it happen.' And the Israelis did just that. All they said was: 'There is a red line in Southern Lebanon, the [River] Litani; the Syrians must not cross it.' The Americans simply transmitted the message to the Syrians: 'Do not cross that red line.'

The Maronites, too, got what they were after. Even with massive military support from the isolationists, the Lebanese State had proved incapable of smashing the Palestinians. The campaign had dragged on for a year, and ever since the hostilities had broken out in the mountains the Maronites were retreating in disorder on all fronts. The Militias of the National Movement, and the Palestinians, were on the verge of crossing the Dhur Choueir-Baskinta-Ouyoune-Simane line[9] and thereby inflicting a decisive defeat on the Maronites. Zahle and Zghorta were also about to fall. In fact, we would not have pushed our advantage any further after that. The isolationists were also very nervous about the intervention of the Syrians – whom they had always seen as Lebanon's main enemy – despite the assurances and guarantees they had received from the United States – and perhaps even from France (the Syrian Minister Khaddam had flown to Paris on several occasions). Syria was constantly having to calm Christian apprehensions about the formation of a 'Greater Syrian' federation.

The Syrians, on the other hand, resented us – myself in particular, because

I had instigated the battle in the Mountain, the sole aim of which was to cut the Gordian knot and put an end to the dirty trench warfare in Beirut. By doing so, we had embarrassed everybody. But the Syrian President misunderstood our intentions. He did not accept that we would not agree to the 'immediate cease-fire' he had demanded of us during my last visit to Damascus, where, during a meeting which lasted for over eight hours, he and I expressed completely divergent viewpoints. He tried to tell us about the pressures which were being exerted upon him. Perhaps we did not take them enough into account: the stakes in the struggle in Lebanon, which had become offensive instead of defensive, were too important for us; we could not let slip by this historic opportunity finally to transform these confessional and outdated institutions into truly secular and democratic ones.

A revolution is an unforgiving affair: the propitious moment has to be seized immediately victory comes within your reach. True, there is something adventuristic about the whole thing, but then, life itself is a calculated and deliberate adventure. Who can determine what part chance and free will play in everyday life? Historical materialism tells us, rightly, that causality must always be taken into account: but the fact remains that men take their decisions through an intuition of freedom which is incumbent upon all real statesmen, as opposed to mere politicians.

At the time, our adventure was calculated as follows: the isolationists had been denied an American military intervention; Mr. Dean Brown had notified us that he had replied negatively to requests from Gemayel, Shamun, etc., and that the international situation had changed since 1958, when American Marines had disembarked in Lebanon. Perhaps every democracy is saddled with a feeling of guilt at the prospect of direct military intervention, whatever theories of imperialism may say. Nor could France be counted on to defend the privileges of a fundamentalist and presumptuous Maronitism. Much water has passed under the bridge since 1860.[10] In any case, we would not have had anything to fear from a French intervention in keeping with the principles of General de Gaulle's policies. While not welcoming it, we would at least have been sure that civil liberties and human rights in Lebanon would not have been jeopardized, and that some form of democracy, however halting, would have survived. Perhaps we were over-hasty when we rejected the proposed military intervention formulated by President Giscard d'Estaing during his visit to the United States, but it was American intentions of which we were suspicious, not French policy. Indeed, throughout the Lebanese crisis, France's attitude was understanding (when possible!), dignified and benevolent.

Some may accuse me of excessive Francophilia and, in a way, they would be right. But I also appreciate the British — when they are being British — and all other peoples who are true to the *sui generis* spirit of their national and moral context. I care less for states that either seek to be something they are not, or act in a manner not their own. In this sense, I feel that the British and the Germans are no longer quite true to themselves: a transatlantic element has crept in. American ways may be good for America, but not for other nations. Europe, including France, runs the risk of losing touch with what it is, what it has been.

To return to our analysis: Israel, according to our calculations, could not intervene without upsetting the whole laboriously constructed edifice, put together, piece by piece, by the Americans and a few Arab States, as part of the build-up to Geneva. At first, the Israelis had no intention of offering their assistance to the isolationists in Lebanon anyway. It was only later that the Syrian military intervention encouraged them to send weapons – or more weapons – to the Falangists, Shamun, Kassis and the others. Israeli military spokesmen, statesmen and the press merely lamented the fact that the isolationists had been dropped by everybody. America may have been vaguely concerned for their fate, but could not accept their claims. Europe looked on from afar, interested and sympathetic, but incapable of understanding the behaviour, still less the motives, of the isolationist Maronites. 1860 was long past, democracy and Europeanization had proceeded steadily, the imperial spirit had gone.

In short, we had every reason to feel confident. Sheikh Bechir Gemayel[11] came to present his condolences when my sister was assassinated by the isolationists amongst whom she had insisted on living. 'We accept your programme of constitutional reform,' he said, 'but in many ways we find that it does not go far enough.' Both sides had only one wish: to begin the negotiations. The end of the conflict seemed imminent. Only Rabin, Peres, Mordecai Gur and other personalities of the Zionist State, gave it to be understood that the events in Lebanon were not over yet, that the Dantesque struggle would continue. According to their own press, the Zionists were acting 'skilfully and with great circumspection'. As for us, just as we felt that the war was coming to an end, that everybody was going to come together at the round table and that peace was about to return, the Syrian Army began its slow but inexorable advance towards Beirut, Saida and Tripoli. Bit by bit, the country was being seized.

Why? For Syria, it was mainly a question of prestige. The Damascus regime could not withdraw without some loss of face, it was already too closely involved. It had set out to teach the Palestinian Liberation Movement a lesson and to bring the left and a rebel Islam to heel. The Syrians wanted to see 'their solution' to the Lebanese problem enforced, not the programme of the Lebanese National Movement. In short, they wanted to impose the 'constitutional message' of President Frangie, which contained only a few timid reforms and a decree affecting journalists, under the fallacious pretext of making them more responsible and independent.

But first, 'Philip of Macedon's' armies had to occupy Beirut. Everything encouraged them to do so: the *Voice of Israel,* the whisperings and hints of the U.S. State Department, even the traditional Muslim politicians of Tripoli and Beirut, who had been taken aback by the growing political influence of the Lebanese National Movement.

Despite his country's desire for prestige, President Assad is not an adventurous man. The Syrian regime only moved in once the acquiescence or support of all the interested parties had been secured, along with Israel's silence (apart from the warning not to cross the Litani). After each military thrust had penetrated two or three kilometres deeper into Lebanon, the troops would stop whilst the politicians in Damascus sounded out the attitudes of the great powers. Tirelessly, the regime sought to calm all fears and deflect all suspicion as its armies steadily gnawed away at the national territory of Lebanon. The Syrian Minister of Foreign Affairs regularly flew to France, to Saudi Arabia, to the Gulf, to Jordan, etc. Permanent contacts with the United States were established. President Tito, ever alert and ready to denounce international infringements of the rights of peoples to self-determination, felt he should have some explanation of the Syrian regime's dubious actions in Lebanon; hence President Assad's stop-over in Belgrade on his return from Paris.

Only the Soviet Union seemed disquieted by events in Lebanon. Articles in *Pravda* and *Izvestia,* and declarations of the Novosti Press Agency reflected this concern, as did the personal letters exchanged by President Assad and General Secretary Brezhnev, and Mr Kosygin's visit to Damascus. The Soviet Prime Minister had to wait two days in the Syrian capital before being granted an interview with President Assad. The penetration of Syrian troops into Lebanese territory had begun only two days before his arrival. By keeping him waiting, Assad sought to assert his independence and the fact that Syrian interests took precedence over any considerations of international law. The Russians betrayed no reaction to this slight; probably the Syrians felt that as they were the very last bastion of the Soviet alliance in the Middle East, it was unlikely that the Russians would prefer the 'democratic victory' of the Lebanese National Movement over the interests of a partner in whom they had invested so much, notably a heavy flow of arms of all sorts and a great deal of technical assistance. And, as always, Geneva was on the horizon and had to be anticipated. My own view is that in this case the Soviets made a mistake. By instituting a broader representative democracy in Lebanon, the political victory of the Lebanese National Movement would have contributed to changing the Arab regimes and would have improved and reinforced Arab-Soviet relations.

The Syrian regime committed the same error of judgement. In the name of immediate gain and illusory interests (as the future was to show) the Syrian leaders sacrificed the democratic emancipation of a whole people, an emancipation which would have acted as a powerful lever for the development of democracy and real socialism throughout the Middle East. Of course, it is open to question whether the Syrian leaders would have welcomed such developments . . . . It would seem that, on the contrary, they found the prospect alarming. In Ba'athist circles in Damascus the word was that 'Kamal Joumblatt is a dangerous man, far more dangerous than Camille Shamun and all the others. He is going to drag us into a new confrontation with Israel.' This was, of course, quite absurd, a truly stupid argument betraying a complete lack of dialectical understanding.

One may well ask whether all these 'progressive' Arab regimes really do wish to institute democracy or socialism. Even on the economic level, the answer remains uncertain. What is this class of millionaires (property speculators, bank and hotel directors, importers, etc.) that is forming? Our independence, our views on representative political democracy, socialism and social economy frightened everybody. So did our tendency to remain independent on the subject of Arabism, and our conception of federal unity on Indian, Swiss or American lines, which has nothing in common with the phony projects for 'Arab unity' launched from time to time by the rulers of the day to beguile the peoples' expectations. What can one say about these prefabricated schemes for co-operation, geared entirely to the achievement of some politically tawdry goal on the international level, or conceived in order to get oneself out of temporary difficulties, to protect oneself provisionally against this or that antagonistic State, or simply to provide oneself with yet another opportunity to indulge in the rhetoric of unity without ever moving closer towards it? Gold and dross, the real and the counterfeit, sincerity and pharisaism, are so inextricably mixed in the baffling jumble of Arab politics. It is so disheartening. And in the background, the constant fear that somebody will do better, will overtake you: the tribal ego, the partisan ego, the national ego.

Anybody with a little analytical ability and some sense of future prospects would have understood what we were trying to do in Lebanon. All that was required of our friends abroad and of the Syrian leaders was a tiny spark of daring. A revolutionary without that spark is no longer a revolutionary. The lack of this spirit of adventure has become the cardinal sin of most Communist regimes and parties, and even more so of the supposedly progressive regimes of the Arab world. The people have been gagged in the name of socialism. Governments have become mesmerized by the mirage of Geneva — a mirage sustained both by the Americans and the Soviet Union — and by the 'agreements' of these two great powers. In Syria especially, the leadership proved incapable of the imaginative effort that a spirit of adventure demands. In 1967, a little revolutionary daring, or — as I would put it — a sense of what revolution calls for, would have transformed the battle of the Golan into an Arab Verdun, a great myth and marker in the pages of history. Instead, it ended in a bloodless retreat from positions which could have been held for months. If only there had been a Syrian Joffre! It is only through meeting such historical challenges that the 'progressive' Syrian regime can truly protect itself. The entire Syrian nation would have rallied round. But the spirit was absent at the rendezvous with history, and the Lebanese adventure (which seemed so unadventurous to us, given the stage our struggle had reached) seemed to interest nobody. On the contrary, it seemed to disturb the bourgeois quiescence of the 'fraternal states'.

This is the second point I wanted to make. Whether in Damascus or in Riyadh, there was only vague and distant interest in the Lebanese problem. The mirage of recovering the territories occupied by Israel remained to the forefront. The general attitude was 'Oh no, not Lebanon again.' When, just after the hostilities had begun, the Arab Front for the Support of the

Palestinian Revolution met in Damascus, the representative of the Syrian
Ba'ath Party even neglected to provide any detailed analysis of the crisis
or to indicate his support for the aims of the Lebanese National Movement.
He preferred instead to go on and on, complaining about the Sinai Agreements. In the end, however, our point of view was endorsed, thanks to all
the other Arab parties.

The third point which must be taken into account in any analysis of the
Syrian leaders' attitude to the Lebanese crisis, is the personal character of
President Assad himself, who evinced such pained humanitarian sympathy
for the victims of the bloody conflict in Lebanon. President Assad seemed
utterly sincere as he bewailed the cruelty and destructiveness of the combat
and expressed the urgent wish to bring it to an end. It was a worthy senti-
ment, which we shared. Nonetheless, it was no excuse for forgetting what
this sewer of blood, ferocity, destruction and shame was all about: the liberation, unification, Lebanization and Arabization of the Lebanese people. But
perhaps there was an underlying misunderstanding: subconsciously, the
Ba'athist Government in Damascus could not bring itself to recognize our
struggle, the struggle of the national movement, as a real revolution: no doubt
because the Ba'ath, in Lebanon, had very little influence and even less
popular support. Our struggle was a genuine democratic revolution, akin to
what happened in Algeria and South Yemen; this may have frightened the
Syrian leaders, who had come to power by a military coup. One might as
well admit that a successful popular revolution in Lebanon would have cast
umbrage upon the progressive military regimes of the region.

I had advised President Assad very frankly:

> I beg you to withdraw the troops you have sent into Lebanon. Carry
> on with your political intervention, your mediation, your arbitration.
> You were about to succeed, one might even say you have succeeded
> already. But you want unanimity and that is impossible. The two
> sides both want peace now and an agreement is imminent. Your
> political arbitration will then be even more unlikely to be effective.
> But I must advise you against military means. We do not want to be a
> satellite state. We want to be independent. We do not want the sort
> of federation preached by your Ba'ath Party representatives in Beirut.
> In any case, the Israelis would eventually turn upon such a federation;
> perhaps they will conquer large areas of Southern Lebanon (the
> Israeli intervention has already begun; Christian enclaves are being set
> up along the frontier) in order to create the secure frontiers they want,
> leaving you with only a part of Lebanon and with a Maronite state
> somewhere in the Mountain. Or else they will attack you directly,
> because a 'Greater Syria' is a danger to Israel. Furthermore, Europe
> will not welcome this partition of our little country, like some new
> Poland or Czechoslovakia.

But I later added:

Do not think we are opposed to the Arab union, on the contrary. We are the only party to have presented a rational federative programme and constitution to all the Arab leaders — but we want a federation which guarantees us our freedom. We do not want the great Syrian prison. When you have moved towards political democracy in Syria, when you have created a real democracy on Western lines, then we will be the first to ask that Lebanon become part of a Syrian-Lebanese federation.

Perhaps my tone vexed him a little, but it was what we had been saying to everybody. Every time I had been to Egypt to meet President Sadat, an old friend from the days when he was President of the Islamic Congress and later of the Afro-Asian movement, I had always stressed the importance we attached to the democratization of Egypt, and of the whole Arab Middle East. In fact President Sadat has already taken steps towards liberalization. There are three parties in the new Chamber, or, at least, three fractions of the same party, a left, a centre and a right. A measure of freedom has already been granted to the Egyptian press. I feel that if Egypt moves towards democracy, we will be able to sustain our own Lebanese democracy, despite the press censorship laws that Syria has imposed upon us. Kuwait too, will, I hope, eventually restore the principle of freedom of speech. It is such a pity that the Emir, made anxious by some of his partners in the Arabian peninsula, has suspended democracy in his small but promising principality. If Syria were to take into account her real interests, the regeneration of Arabism, the renaissance of ideas and the will to healthy revolution in the Arab world, she too would embark upon a course of political democratization, as would Iraq, Sudan and the great Arab countries of Africa.

In passing, it is worth mentioning that Israel, through its Prime Minister, Mr. Rabin, and its Chief of Staff, General Gur, was announcing the storm nearly three months before it arrived. 'There will be trouble in Lebanon, the Lebanese will be fighting each other and fighting the Palestinians' said the prophetic and provocative voices. 'It is in Lebanon that we will avenge ourselves upon the Palestinians, not directly but by fanning a civil war against them.' And so it came to pass. We were always careful to listen to the declarations and remarks of the Israeli authorities, in order to find out what was going to happen, rather as one listens to the weather forecast. When they said 'There is going to be a lull in the fighting', we knew we would have time to bandage our wounded, as happened on several occasions during this long conflict. When they said that hostilities were going to break out again with renewed violence, we were sure the war was about to continue.

The attitude of the Soviet Union was, to be honest, not very clear. As I have already mentioned, the U.S.S.R. hesitated to take sides, understandably enough; the problems of Lebanon seemed enormously complex to all of us. Obviously, the Soviet Union was aware that the first truly promising democratic movement of the left in the Arab world had just emerged in Lebanon. Perhaps the Soviets had doubts about our over-democratic tendencies concerning political institutions. But nowadays, many parties throughout the world, including some communist parties, strongly criticize Moscow's interpretation of Marxist socialism. The French and Italian Communist Parties are notable examples. In many countries, the concept of the new historical bloc,[12] has, in practice, often replaced a system which, until recently, had been based exclusively on the proletariat; the principle of the dictatorship of the revolutionary authorities has also been extensively challenged. At most, it is granted that such a dictatorship may justify a highly authoritarian government, provided essential human rights and civil liberties are respected. These rights and liberties are an inestimably important gain in man's historical struggle both for individual and collective liberation. No revolutionary authority should ever be seen to put the clock back in this domain. Obviously, we still have far to go, but one day all the socialist and communist parties in the world will adopt this standpoint. What use is bread without freedom?

Having said that, the U.S.S.R. undoubtedly approved of the practical and undogmatic spirit of co-operation which linked the Progressive Socialist Party of Lebanon with the Lebanese Communist Party and other left groups. Our revolutionary pragmatism and our calculated spirit of adventure may have made them a little nervous, just as they were not without problems for our old friend President Assad, and a number of other leaders in the Arab world who have opted for socialism, as if by accident . . . but that is another story. In any case, our friendship towards the U.S.S.R. and the communist world was unfailing. We seemed about to contaminate all the progressive countries of the Arab world with the virus of freedom. Perhaps we could even rouse the slumbering giant of Arab nationalism, and inspire the people with that spirit of emancipation which alone can save the Arab world from the political stagnation induced by tyranny. Our resolutely independent stance, our way of taking a tilt at whoever we saw fit, irrespective of that spirit of compromise which rules the Arab world, and which constitutes the essence of the agreement with the two super-powers, seemed likely to radicalize Arab opinion concerning the projected solution of the Israeli-Arab-Palestinian conflict. We threatened to unfasten the straitjacket imposed by the autocratic and military — I will not say fascist — regimes of the Arab world. Once contaminated with our aspiration to political freedom, that Arab world, now slumped in the stupor induced by the opium of the ruling ideologies, and quietly asphyxiated by the noxious fumes of opportunism and compromise, would be in a position to demand the complete implementation of the 1947 U.N. resolution: the return, with full political rights, of all the Palestinian refugees to their homes in Israel, and the establishment of a Palestinian State on 46% of the territory of historic Palestine. Everything would thus be thrown into question, from the proposed tiny West Bank state (20 or 25% of historic Palestine) to the Geneva Conference itself.

The U.S.S.R. constantly advised us to remain on good terms with Syria, whilst maintaining our close relations with the Palestinian revolution. In their eyes this triple alliance constituted the best guarantee of peace and progress in this area of the Levant. For a long time, such was indeed our policy, although we never broke off our links with Egypt, Iraq and the other Arab countries. We dropped this policy only when the Syrian attitude towards the Lebanese National Movement changed, suddenly and, to us, inexplicably, even if we had long been the *enfant terrible* of the region. The Progressive Socialist Party was no longer endlessly droning on about imperialism in every speech, in that manner so typical of superficial ideologies. Our socialist and communist friends had also rid themselves of this kind of linguistic bigotry. When we needed to talk about imperialism we preferred to refer to the United States, or the other powers concerned, by name.

The U.S.S.R. apparently did everything in its power to calm the Syrian leaders, to bring them round to our point of view, and later to defuse their anger towards us when we refused to be mere pawns on the chess-board of the Arab world and withheld our consent to the latest Syrian armistice proposal — although we never rejected these proposals outright, as all our friends will testify. We simply insisted that the Lebanese were better qualified to deal with the problems of Lebanon than the Syrians. Obviously we hoped that one day the Soviets would support us more energetically. We expected them to take a firmer, more principled and more definite stance, especially when the troops of 'Philip the Syrian' began to cross our frontiers. In our conversations we would sometimes jokingly quote the comparison between the Soviets and the polar bear: the polar bear is slow to shake itself awake, but once it is on the move, it is best to keep out of its way. Everybody knows how deeply Lenin was attached to the 'principle of the right of peoples to self-determination'.

As a people with a love of myths — the Arabs are the great protagonists of the myth in today's world — we dearly hoped to see the Russian mythos hammering on the table, standing up to everybody else and telling the Syrians 'No, No, and No!' Without that traditional Russian mysticism (Lenin called it the Russian revolutionary spirit) how could communism have been established in the U.S.S.R.? So the mystic in all of us (surely socialism, communism and Arab nationalism are amongst the great myths of our era) had great expectations of the Russian mythos. Almost every week we were sending political manifestos and information on recent developments to the Soviets. Our conversations with their representatives were always lucid and frank. A member of the Political Bureau of the Lebanese Communist Party even went to Moscow, and the French Communist Party intervened on our behalf.

In the end, the U.S.S.R.'s position concerning the Syrians became relatively less accommodating, but it never attained that principled firmness we had hoped for. Perhaps we had been too idealistic — or too naive, which amounts to the same thing — or perhaps we believed, as every revolutionary is entitled to believe, that we were the very navel of this part of the world. In any case, the game was worth the candle. But the Syrians had different views; they felt they could behave as the U.S.S.R.'s favourite children, especially after the loss of Soviet influence in Sadat's Egypt.

The Russians are a sentimental people; they had been deeply affronted by the Egyptian volte-face, and were not prepared to just let it pass by, even though such an attitude cost them dearly in terms of their diplomacy and policy in the Arab world. One should never forget that Egypt is the best understood country in the Middle East and the most amply provided for with arms and capital. It remains a primordial axis and a powerful centre of polarization in the framework of the Arab world — and even of Africa. Sadat's Egypt, too, should have been more patient and more understanding. The Soviets are a great world power and their foreign interests are as much a source of concern to them as is the Siberian Third World; oil capital is as important to them as the 'electricity' referred to by Lenin.

The Soviet Union's position in the Middle East continues to be an uncomfortable one, and once again the blame lies with our Saudi friends and their exaggerated fear of communism. In this instance, the mystical spirit of the Arabs is acting against the true interests of the Arab peoples. In practice, American pragmatism is drawing the most benefit from this estrangement. and giving little in return; Marxist communism, on the other hand, is changing, slowly but steadily. A more abrupt and definitive change can be expected reasonably soon. Freedom will surely win out in the end, borne aloft by the new and numerous ranks of the intelligentsia, by the scientists, the artists, the intellectuals, by cultured people at all levels, and finally, by the mass of the citizens themselves.

The Soviets, who have brought us so much, deserved a little more gratitude in return. Elementary decency required it. No state or empire in history has had at its disposal so much money, power, energy and prestige as these Arab oil States, and no government or State in history has used it so badly. It would have been to their honour had they used this wealth to eliminate poverty, underdevelopment and misery in Egypt, Yemen, the Sudan and elsewhere in Africa and Asia. Hundreds of millions of disinherited people throughout the world are waiting to be delivered from hunger by the petrodollars. I am talking about a massive and systematic aid programme, not the miserable few farthings which have been dispensed like crumbs from the banqueting tables. Let there be an end to the shameful spectacle of these Arab billionaires, who live like inhuman madmen, spending their money with the profligacy of a Tiberius or a Vespasian dining on mounds of larks' tongues. This gold, which so many people need, disgraces the Arabs in the eyes of every man of conscience, Arab or not. What a powerful lever all that gold and oil could have been for the peaceful, if not military, liberation of all Palestine and the creation of an Arab-Jewish federation throughout the Promised Land.

As it is, Europe and America have abdicated their role and set aside the essential principles of international law in order to pursue a policy of self-interest *a la* Metternich. The Soviet Union thus stands out as the only guarantor of an independent Lebanon, the faithful support of the Palestinian movement and the champion of national liberation movements throughout the world, including the Lebanon. We must have been a most troublesome protege. Nonetheless, articles in *Pravda* and *Izvestia* constantly encouraged and cheered us, even if the Soviet Union ignored our requests for one small ship loaded with foodstuffs to break the Israeli and Syrian naval blockade which was cutting us off from our supplies. In our naive simplicity, what we pressed for most of all was a firm and clear declaration of principle by the Soviet Government, some sort of memorandum which would have put an end to the Syrian invasion. The reader should bear in mind that we felt abandoned by everybody and that the land we had liberated was being reduced to a field of ashes.

The Soviet Union allowed this situation to develop: every great nation is, in the end, a prisoner of its immediate national interests. But the Soviet Union's real interest would have been to support us completely, first to assert a principle and secondly to encourage the gradual emergence in the Lebanon of the first free socialist society. We could have been the lever by which the Soviets could have changed the face of the Arab world, won back the lost friendship of many Arab states and consolidated their relationships of co-operation in the Middle East. Moderate and democratic socialism in Lebanon would have represented the promise of true revolution throughout the Arab countries, because it would have been the fruit of a genuine socialist revolt of the people, as opposed to all the military juntas and neo-fascist regimes of right and left. The Russians, the Europeans and the Americans, could all only benefit by supporting political democracy in the Middle East, instead of all these clumsy unstable pseudo-socialist or neo-fascist military Arab regimes, that can never be either socialist or democratic.

True to tell, I do not know whether the Soviet Union genuinely wishes to see socialism implanted in the region. But if the U.S.S.R. had really decided to protect the right of a people to self-determination, by outspokenly opposing any invasion of our territory, what could the Syrians have done about it? All their weapons come from the Soviet Union, and they were nearly $4 billion in debt to the Russians. Sadly, the U.S.S.R. did not realize that Syrian policy had already moved halfway to the other side.

So did the plot succeed in all its aims? I think not. The Lebanese and the Palestinian resistance are not yet disarmed, and public opinion still has to be gagged, since freedom of speech and democracy in Lebanon would constitute permanent impediments to any partial solutions to the Palestinian problem.

The plot continues, with the aim of stabilizing the regime in Damascus and in the other countries that are preparing to sell out the Palestinian cause. On the horizon one can distinguish the ominous outlines of the Geneva Conference and an eventual partition of Lebanon.

Notes

1. The start of the Lebanese Civil War.
2. Usual meeting place of the Maronite right during the crisis.

3. The first inter-confessional conflict, which was halted by the American military intervention.
4. The Falangist leader.
5. The movement of the Lebanese left as a whole, presided over by Kamal Joumblatt.
6. On the occasion of the Riyadh and Cairo agreements (October 1976) the Arab states jointly approved Syria's military intervention in Lebanon (April 1976).
7. The presidential palace.
8. A Syrian-sponsored Palestinian organization.
9. The line of hills which dominate the sector held by the conservatives, north-east of Beirut.
10. In 1860 Napoleon III sent an expeditionary force to protect the Christians.
11. The son of the Fhalangist leader.
12. A reference to that put forward by Roger Garady.

2. Once upon a time, the Druses . . .

'Behind every trough, there is the crest of a new wave surging forth.'

I am Druse. Our roots in Lebanon lie in Moukhtara, a little village in the Chouf where my family's palace is situated. Here, I am often called 'the lord of Moukhtara', sometimes a little ironically, as if there were some contradiction with my position as a progressive leader. I accept the epithet but not the intentions behind it: one must be a lord in the real sense of the term, lord of one's own life.

Perched up there on its rock, Moukhtara is a residence which has been built in stages over two and a half centuries. When our ancestors left Northern Syria, they first settled at Muzraat-el-Chouf, where they found refuge in a little cave. Shortly before, one of our ancestors, Emir Janboulad (the Kurdish name of the family) had carved himself out a little kingdom in the north of Syria, which included Homs, Hama, Aleppo, Damascus and part of Anatolian Turkey. He managed to retain his independence for several years and signed treaties with the Vatican, the Grand Duchy of Tuscany, Spain and the small Christian States of that time. In exchange, he was given political and military support, weapons and a few cannon. The treaty he signed in 1607 with the Duchy of Tuscany has in fact remained famous in the history of the region. Europe seemed to take a particular interest in this little principality which extended over territories that had consistently been of great strategic importance.

My ancestor, Ali Janboulad, was the first in the East to grant franchises to the Christians of Syria, giving them the same rights and liberties as all the other subjects of the Ottoman Empire. He received ambassadors to his court and struck coinage in his own name. In the end, he was defeated by a Turkish army of 300,000 men, led by the Prime Minister himself, Al-Sadr el Aazam. It was then that he came with his little family to seek refuge in Muzraath el-Chouf.

He had no means at his disposal, since all our properties in Syria had been confiscated. Only the ancestral residence of the Janboulad remained in our hands. Later, one of our 'grandfathers', Rabah Janboulad, married a wealthy woman, the only child of the Kadi family who more or less dominated the entire area, both religiously and socially: they were Druses. When the young girl's father died, Ali Janboulad inherited all his estates, and that was how we began to have a little property in this country.

Another ancestor, Sheikh Ali Janboulad, was later to acquire great influence. He was a wise man who eventually became what is known as the Sheikh of Sheikhs, the dominant Druse religious figure. He was the chief of the four other Druse sheikhs, hence the title Sheikh Akl of the Druses. His authentically Druse manners, his piety and his wisdom, earned him a considerable reputation, which enabled him to exercise a certain political influence. He was, in a way, the arbiter between the princes of the time, the Shehab, who were endlessly quarrelling amongst themselves. From time to time, he managed to bring peace to this Great Chouf Valley where successive waves of Druses have sought refuge over the years.

The first Druse initiates installed themselves in the Wadi Raym, in the Rachaya-Hasbaya region, another great valley at the foot of the Anti-Lebanon. This valley extends southwards from the Bekaa, and it was there that the Druse religion really began to develop. Subsequently, the Druses spread throughout this area of the Chouf, pushing back the Shia Muslims who had preceded them there. As early as the 13th Century, other ancestors had settled the Sinn el-Fil region, near Beirut, and had spread all the way up the high slopes of the Metn and into the Hammana area, occupying both sides of the valley up to Kesruan, past Bikfaya and Beit Mery. They lived there for several decades until the Mamelukes of Wali Ibrahim Pasha of Egypt swept through the region and massacred them. That was in 1585: 60,000 Druses were killed. But during the same period others had gained a foothold in the Gharb region – the west – around Aleppo. They had been gradually infiltrating the Mountain ever since around the year 1000.

Our family began to reign in Lebanon in the era of Emir Fakhreddinne, and became more and more powerful from then on. We are not exactly sure when we first converted to the Druse faith. The Druses have a very strict code on the subject; outsiders to the esoteric sect cannot usually become Druses. Apostasy was only possible during the reign of the Fatimid Caliph Al-Hakim Biamrallah, around the year 1000. Later the 'gate' was closed. It thus seems quite probable that our ancestors were already Druses when they were living in the Aley region. That, in fact, would explain the presence of 60,000 Druses in this part of Southern Turkish Anatolia today and the 20,000 Druses in the north of Syria (Djebel el-A'la).

During the era of the Shehab princes, 300 years ago, the Joumblattis began to play an active role in Lebanese politics, but it was already a family tradition. At the same time many of them were also great religious patriarchs. My great grandfather, Sheikh Ali, had acquired such renown for his religious austerity that he was believed to have certain miraculous powers. For instance, pieces of his shirt would be bought for pregnant women to touch, in order to help them in childbirth. Any man who remains true to himself, and to that which we call God, may be able to accomplish some authentic gesture in accordance with his Truth – that is what we usually call a miracle.

During the Shehab era, our ancestors thus played an important role. In a way it was they who governed, through the Shehab Emirs, rather like Richelieu in France. That was enough for them; the title of Emir could only be borne by descendants of the line of Emirs who reigned in Lebanon.

They went through many ups and downs during the history of our little country. Through the Joumblatts and a few other families, the Druses have played a key role in the development of what Father Yoaquim Mobarak calls 'the elaboration of the Lebanese idea'. In fact, this idea, this tendency to independence, is the achievement of the Druses who, as a Muslim sect, could allow themselves a certain freedom *vis-a-vis* Islam and the Ottoman Empire, which enabled them to organize a little state that was relatively independent from the Turkey of that time. Their warlike qualities were also widely respected. The very first foundations of a politically autonomous Lebanon had been laid by the previous Druse dynasties, the Maan and the Tannoukhs, who had reigned since the year 1000.

The great Druse families did not always get on with one another, but rivals were always prepared to come together the moment the issue concerned the fate of the Druses or of the emergent Lebanon. They allowed the Maronites, and the Christians in general, to penetrate the Kesruan, the Metn (to the north of Mount Lebanon), the Aley region and the Chouf, where the Druses constituted the political and military infrastructure. This semi-independent principality was linked to political Islam through a certain obedience owed to the Sublime Porte, but it also enjoyed a considerable autonomy, which fluctuated with the times, the strength or weakness of the Ottoman Empire, and the balance of forces in the region. The Druses played a major part in preserving the area's relative independence. Their function was to defend the coast and protect the ports of Saida, Tyre and Beirut from all foreign attack.

What became known after 1917 as the Grand-Liban was built up around this Druse political concept of a multi-confessional Lebanon, dominated politically by the Druses and the Muslims, a notion of autonomy which had constantly animated the history of the little Arab Emirate. The only difference was that the political system adopted for the 'Grand-Liban' was confessionalist — religious based — rather than secular, and thereby opened the way for the unjustified dominance of the Maronites. And it was a disaster.

The blame rests mainly on the French Mandate. The Maronites may take excellent care of their own affairs, but they are poor managers for a republic. They are too closely bound by their sectarianism, and by a sense of their own interest. As a warrior aristocracy, the Druses had called in the Maronites to work the land in the vast area they controlled; at the time, the Christians in general provided the agricultural workforce and the small traders and artisans in the towns. In those days they were thus the real proletarians in Lebanon, however much they may now wish to reject this line of descent. It was not that the Druses were incapable of engaging in agriculture, but their population was fairly small, especially after the massacres of 1585 — and they thus had to assume a role which far exceeded that which their numbers seemed to warrant. There were not enough Druses to cultivate this land of Lebanon — this Druse Mountain, to give it its historical name.

The Zionists call the Druses 'the fighting minority of the Middle East'. Their whole history is one of internecine wars and struggles with other peoples to preserve this or that principle, or to obtain an alliance with this or that *wali*[1] in Damascus against some other *wali* in Saida. They were the infantry, ever on the alert along the coast. Their political importance stemmed from their warrior role; when the former declined, the latter suffered in consequence.

In Lebanon, the Joumblatts were amongst the first to create political parties which extended throughout the country, from north to south. Their partisans were known as the Joumblatti. The Yazbecki, presided over by the Aamad family of Barouk, were another great Druse party.

This was how the Druse Emirs of the Tannour and Maan dynasties had regrouped their partisans — the Kaissites and Yemenites — in the past, even before the Joumblatts. The pattern may have developed out of a kind of aristocratic coalition, but all the Lebanese people — Christian, Sunni or Shia — considered these parties as the first popular political bodies; membership was drawn from every community, not just from the Druse population. These movements prefigured and promoted a secularization of Lebanese politics which, unfortunately, was disrupted in the middle of the 19th Century by the chauvinistic and destructive eruption of the Maronites upon this promising political scene. It is thus not surprising that there are so many people of liberal inclination amongst the Druses, for all that they retain a great pride in their community and in their religious, cultural and political heritage. They are famous throughout history for their liberal mentality and lack of chauvinism.

The ensuing events of 1842 to 1860 (the Maronite offensive) had much in common with what is happening today: an offensive led by the Maronites, with the clergy at their head, to gain privileges which the Christians had not enjoyed before, notably political power. In 1864, it ended with the dismemberment of Lebanon and the constitution of a little Maronite enclave, the Christian dominated Petit-Liban. The struggle also had a social dimension, in that the farmers and the vast majority of the Maronite peasants sought to emancipate themselves from the Druse yoke. The wars were thus both religious and social but, regrettably, the religious aspect was predominant, hence the eventual partition of the country. After the French intervention to protect the militarily defeated Maronites, 1864 was marked by the break-up of the great Druse estates.

Previously, the Druses owned all the Bekaa, the Metn, the Sahel area of Baadba and a considerable part of Beirut, which was then only a small town with fewer than 16,000 inhabitants. These great estates through which the Druses had predominated were not the only ones to go. 1864 also witnessed the disappearance of what was then known as the Emirate of Lebanon, which had been based entirely on a form of political feudalism. This revolution, or rather this *jacquerie,* later took on a confessional aspect only because the Maronite political leaders pushed it in that direction, towards that ravine from which Lebanon has since been unable to emerge.

What died in 1864 was the basic underlying structure of the Lebanese ideal of a liberal and dynamic Lebanon embroiled in all the affairs of the Middle East, fighting here and there in every war and with a finger in every political pie in the region. Lebanon lost both the activism of its foreign policy and its internal structure of freedom for all its citizens. These were replaced by the narrow sectarianism of Maronite confessionalism. The fighting Emirate had to make way for a miniature Lebanon, a Christian shelter for 'psychological refugees'. We have lived with this nationally deformed idea to this day. When they disembarked upon our shores, the French forgot to bring with them the principles of their great revolution of 1789. They were content to maintain a status quo they had already done a great deal to establish.

The Druses have never needed protection. Nonetheless, some of them entertained fairly good relations with the French, and based their power first on the French and then on an admittedly fairly large section of the Druse people. This Maronite support for the Druses was geared to reviving an historical alliance, in order to create the political basis for the new Lebanese state. As a result the Grand-Liban was reassembled out of its old traditions and through the political will of General Gouraud, Patriarch Hoyek and a few Maronite leaders of the time, such as Emile Edde and Bechara el-Khoury. Although geographically larger, the new Lebanon revolved primarily around the need to preserve, indirectly, the Maronite enclave of the Petit-Liban. This politico-religious enclave was protected by means of certain discriminatory practices affecting political representation, notably the system of national representation. The French, who sought only to maintain their presence along the coast, were the real culprits. All our present woes stem from this political confessionism, and recent events are merely the reverse of what happened in 1842-60; what we have now is a crusade by all patriotic Muslims and Christians for the secularization of the Lebanese state, the elimination of political confessionalism and the establishment of a unitary state on a civilian foundation. As far as we are concerned, the events of 1975 and 1976 are a sort of 1789 revolution against what happened in 1859, but within a Lebanese idiom, horror mixed with heroism. Indeed, the present divisions into religious and political communities recall the old division into orders which prevailed in France under the *ancien regime:* the clergy, the aristocracy and the third estate. The third estate and the petty bourgeoisie are in revolt against the reigning Maronite *haute bourgeoisie.*

In less than a century, the Druses fell from a dominant to a dominated position. Throughout history, they had played a role out of all proportion to their numbers. This *tour de force* was only possible because they were then a proud, organized, dynamic and warlike nation. One should always bear in mind that they represented the Greek sense of order, having inherited, in their holy books and secrets, the whole philosophy of Pythagoras, Socrates, Plato and neo-Platonism. One might add that the Ottomans had always relied on the Druse feudal structure to govern the country indirectly.

Democratic ideas spread after Bonaparte's arrival in the Levant and, in particular, with the setting up of missionary schools and the establishment of the Saint Joseph University by the Jesuits and of the American University. The Christians then began to be aware of their new strength within the ailing Ottoman Empire and started to acquire a Western culture. The emergence of a new Christian intelligentsia contributed enormously to the political changes which were to follow.

In the meanwhile, the country's economy was also evolving. As elsewhere, the traditional agricultural economy was gradually transformed into an economy based on trade, crafts and markets, through which the bourgeoisie rose to become the dominant class. The silk and tobacco industries flourished and the spinning mills grew apace. This economic development was further accelerated when Beirut was linked to Damascus by a railway and a usable road. The financial and commercial bourgeoisie also did well. The port of Beirut was enlarged and subsequently became the main outlet for the Syrian interior. The Maronites established themselves in the centre of Lebanon, in the two Metn and in the Chouf. All these economic and demographic changes paved the way for a new political regime. Furthermore, the political and financial support given to the Maronites by Europe, and by France in particular, acted as a catalyst which accelerated the emergence of a new social, economic and political situation.

No account of the history of the country would be complete without some mention of the contribution made by the Druses and the Joumblatt family — the most powerful members of this political and warrior aristocracy. Let us begin with Moukhtara. Its name means 'the Elect Village', 'the Chosen One', which is strangely reminiscent of the name given to a small town in the south of Iraq, Al-Moukhtara, which was the focal point of the great social revolution waged by the *Zunjs*, the black slaves. It is said that the uprising was inspired by the teachings of the great sufis and in particular by those of the famous Al-Hallaj. I do not know why my little village was given the name Al-Moukhtara nor what relation it might have with its namesake in the Persian Gulf.

The German Baedeker claims that our house (*dar*, in Arabic) was built on the site of an old crusader castle. The Joumblatt family once possessed all the lands of Aley up to the Chouf. The great Druse families owned all the big estates, one village, two villages, ten villages . . . from the Kesruan frontier to Jezzine and beyond, from the sea to the Syrian frontier and, at one time, even to the outskirts of Damascus. Now, we only have about 30 or 35 hectares around Moukhtara. We also had a substantial estate by the sea, but we have given most of it to the tenants who farmed it. We may still be the biggest landowners in Moukhtara, but everybody who lives there owns a little land. The other remaining great estate in the area belongs to the Hasn el-Dine Sheikhs, who used to fulfil the role of viceroys for the Joumblatts.

The village of Moukhtara is half Christian, half Druse, which bears witness to the welcome offered to the Christians by our ancestors. Some Christians were even responsible for the administration of the Joumblatt's domains and assisted them in their political tasks. The Druse lords found them to be intelligent, willing, and perhaps more culturally advanced than others. In any case a true symbiosis was established between the great religious communities of the country, the Christians, Druses, Sunnis and Shias.

On Sundays, in our house, the people of the neighbouring area come to greet us and to ask questions: 'What is new, how are the politics going . . .' In a way, I am their talking newspaper, the columnist they need. They sometimes come to consult us about their personal problems, the projects they would like to carry out in the village, even their medical problems. They expect a great deal from me. As I am their parliamentary representative and have a little influence in the state, they rely on me to build this or that school, a particular road, a new water pipe: in short, to deal with everything which concerns public services. And then there are the family matters about which they come for advice. They trust me. Others come from abroad, out of curiosity. There is a certain dignity to Druse esotericism, which is a mixture of wisdom and realism. We are a people with 5,000 years of history behind us and we trace our line back to Hermes Trimegistes, whom we call Imkopeh. Socrates, Pythagoras and Plato are widely read in our little country; people greet each other with 'peace be upon him', '*Al salam alaih*'. In short it is a kind of tiny humanist Greece, an *agora* in which people take an interest in everything.

Apart from the domain of Moukhtara we also have a property of 400 hectares (188 acres) by the sea, but it yields very little because there is almost no water for the fields and no money to invest in them. Distant properties are usually badly managed, there are so many other things to do . . . and, personally, money does not interest me. As soon as I have a little, I try to get rid of it as quickly as possible. I know how these bits of paper can stick to one's fingers. Money can become a pernicious microbe if it is not used to help others. Property equals social function. I use it as economically as possible, spending only the bare minimum necessary for personal needs, so that the surplus may always go to others. I am content to live as an honest man amongst the common folk. Mean with oneself, generous to others; a neighbour in need is as a brother, and stands as a symbol for God Himself. That is the Druse way.

Actually, Moukhtara provides a living for only a handful of people. There is a manager, a gamekeeper and a few labourers who work the land from time to time. In all, about ten people. The olive trees are not as fruitful as they used to be and olive oil is increasingly running into competition from other vegetable oils, those awful hydrogenated products such as groundnut oil . . . . And our orchard is no longer profitable. In practice, I live mainly on my parliamentary salary. The produce of our lands feeds very few people. We have no train of servants: only a cook and a cleaner. I am not as rich as has been suggested. I would like to have been, so that I could have shared it out and set an example to the wealthy of this world. I believe one should live modestly, because in the end it is the simple life which brings happiness. The privileged few are only the managers of the rest. Whether one has great estates or not, anything above that which is needed for necessary expenditure should be given to others. I do not believe in this absurd and ugly consumer society; men who live within it will end by consuming themselves.

One day there will surely have to be land reform in Lebanon, which will do away with the big estates and enable each Lebanese to own his own small plot of land. I myself have distributed 100 hectares to my tenants at Sibline, by the sea, and it was a source of real joy both for them and me. Big estates are unnatural, they distort the meaning of ownership: everybody likes to own something, it acts as an extension of people's senses, their hands, their bodies, their personalities. One of our party's demands is 'Every Lebanese a Landowner'. Small or medium landholdings change people's attitudes and help them adopt a more independent, dignified and responsible stance towards the authorities. A sense of responsibility and a love of freedom go hand in hand with possession of land.

Who are the Druses? Our dogma is based on initiation; only the initiates know how to read and understand the holy books that we call the Books of Wisdom. It is an extension of the Greek and Egyptian hermetic schools – the esoteric traditions – which have passed into Muslim Sufism. At present only a Druse who has known 'the message' in a previous life can be initiated, if he is worthy. But one should remember that, according to the tradition and established belief, the Druses, which is to say the adepts of Unity – the Vedantists in a way – exist under different names in all the great religions of the world and thus represent more than one quarter of humankind. A new cycle of initiation will begin around the year 2000 with a message from God, the appearance of a great sage. Then the road will be opened again. People throughout the world will be able to set out along it, towards the true goal of all human life, knowledge of the Truth and its realization.

Strictly speaking, I am not a religious leader, but I have studied Drusism sufficiently to be able to offer some analyses. I really came to understand it through the teachings of the Indian *vedanta advaita* and the philosophy of the Greeks, which enabled me to discover the key to the Druse mysteries, for our gnosticism is the same as that one finds throughout the world, most notably amongst the great sages of India and classical antiquity. My knowledge gives me a certain spiritual, but not religious, authority. The sheikhs[2] and the initiates come to see me; we pray together and sometimes we meditate. I read them old texts of Hindu *advaita* thought, very strictly elaborated in India over the ages, and explain to them the essential ideas of this historical and human spiritual endeavour. The local initiates are inspired by these readings. I myself was taught in India by a great sage who is my Pythagoras and Socrates. The Druses hold that the first manifestation (*tegeli*) of the Most High (*el-Ali*) took place in the (imaginary?) town of Jim Matchin in India a million years ago. Westerners count in thousands of years – we count in millions and tens of millions of years.

Dr. Roger Godel, a man of science deeply familiar with Ancient Greece, has written some very important books concerning this liberating experience. (He was a friend of Jung's, the famous psychologist who also took an interest in the East). There is no hiatus: for him, Greek wisdom and Hindu wisdom form a single whole. The *Vedanta,* the hermetic key, opens up all the ancient books of wisdom of this part of the Near East, be it Egyptian antiquity, Greek antiquity or Sufism. The light of *Advaita* illuminates the teachings of Plato, Socrates, Plotinus and the other masters of antiquity, including Heraclitus. Indeed, for the last eight years I have been working on a book on Heraclitus which I intend to publish shortly.

The Druse religion preaches the essential unity of all things and all beings, the substantive unity of the universe in its physical and spiritual form: rather as if all the elements were seen against the same background, a single noumenon. God, the world and the soul form a single entity. I have contributed to reacquainting my people with this simple and essential unity of which the Druses had rather lost sight over the ages, although it is clearly expressed in their holy books. I have worked for over 12 years to reintroduce them to some of their lost books, which I have had copied from the rediscovered originals by initiated scribes. A handwritten book has much more 'psychic power' than a printed volume. The effort and intellectual tension contributed by the transcriber gives the words an enormous suggestive power. Human intellect shines forth from the page, as if by magic. The understanding of the writer impregnates the paper itself.

Our religion is a meditative one, and like Ancient Greek philosophy, it ascribes a meaning to life, society and human destiny. Aristotle, one of our sages, states somewhere that the purpose of life is the meditation of Reason. It is not a religion like all the others, a *Shari'a* (law) in the Koranic or Hebrew sense, or a religion based on faith like Christianity or Islam. What matters for the Druse is personal conviction, a vision of internal truth, self knowledge a mind unencumbered by anything in its quest for the absolute. It is a religion of spiritual ascetics, of gnostics committed to ordinary life; a religion of ethics as much as of knowledge. The 'know thyself' which is fundamental to truth is basic to the Druse whose essential quest is for complete genuineness.

I was the first to go to India to complete my spiritual education. Since then, a group of adepts from the Druse Djebel (the Djebel el-Arab, in Syria) has also been there. One of them in fact chose to stay and put on the ochre robe of the *Samnyasin* monks. He decided to remain with one of the great spiritual figures of India, Sai Baba, an extraordinary thaumaturge and miracle worker. I do not know why he works miracles; usually sages endowed with this gift abstain from violating the ordinary laws of nature, whether physical or psychological. Sai Baba says he works miracles almost despite himself, out of benevolence and to help convince people. I have not yet met him personally, although he is still alive. But I have met Shri Atmatanda, whom I have visited eight times, and also Shri Sankarasharga of Kanchipuram. I used to stay for a week, a fortnight, sometimes a month, and I regret not having been able to stay for much longer, for several years even; but there was work to be done at home. Shri Atmatanda's house was an *ashram,* since this sage had not turned his back upon the world. His master, Shri Yogananda, had ordered him not to become *samnyasin.*

I first came to hear of Shri Atmatanda through Roger Godel and his wife, and then through the Hindu writer Raja Rao, who was particularly interested in him. Eventually his disciples in France invited him to Europe, and on his way back, I met him at Cairo Airport for half an hour. It was quite amazing — I did not concentrate on the words he spoke, but the experience was like an exploration of one's own depths, a revelation of the Impersonal in oneself, the Truth within oneself communicating with the Truth within him. I was completely won over — he was so powerful, yet at the same time so simple and humble. I felt he was one of the greatest expressions of India throughout the ages. His works complete the teachings of Adi Shankara, Rama, Krishna and others. His conversation had an extraordinary luminosity. It was as if Ancient Greece itself was speaking . . . When he spoke of Truth, it was as if the Truth within him was surging forth from some hidden wellspring. It was a striking moment of union, that ecstacy of understanding which arises in the presence of a sage: knowledge which transcends both the senses and the intellect; true *samadhi.*[3]

Even without ever having seen him before, I would have recognized him instantly. When someone has achieved Truth, it shines forth from him. As Mahatma Gandhi put it, he becomes genuine, even his body is Truth. These things cannot really be put into words . . . . He seemed different every time I looked at him, like a wave of images passing through his eternity. He reflected that presence of the Unchanging within the flux of sensory, mental and bodily change. It was an inexpressibly direct vision of the Divine, perhaps even a vision of God in human form, or more than God, since while God is the highest conception of the spirit, the sage is the Reality of God; he achieves and expresses this Reality of God, that which is real amidst the unreal, a direct Vision of the True, of Being.

Everything which exists partakes of a divine nature, for in our understanding, the divine exists only in terms of or in contradiction with the material or non-divine. But every being is physically and psychically formed out of this divine substratum. So that when Shri Atmatanda or Ramana Maharishi achieved Truth, their bodies achieved it with them and attained their own Essence; these men barely have a body any more, their body is present to our senses as an image, but is itself beyond all images, as pure Truth shining forth from the Consciousness of Being. These inexpressible things were completely apparent in the presence of Shri Atmatanda that day at Cairo Airport. Even ordinary people must have been intrigued by his presence, even if they were not at all affected by it; his radiance reaches out to everybody and everything. The world is full of sleepwalkers, so few are truly awake. In the presence of the sage, one is awakened to the true Self and can thus be said to be awakened *in* the sage. It is this great Awareness which gives the sages their luminescent aspect. As the legend says, if the sage sits beneath a tree which is almost completely dried up and about to die, the tree will blossom magnificently one last time. Similarly, one can understand how sages can be loved from the first meeting, even if they are, alas, subsequently forgotten.

We Druses have no churches or mosques in the usual sense: instead, there is the *majliss,* the council where the initiates gather each Thursday evening to pray together. But there is no specific place of worship which one must attend: one can just as well pray at home, and one is free to do so. There is also the *khalwa,* a sort of cloister where one isolates oneself from the world in order to pray and meditate. Near here, in the Chouf, we have the *khalwa el-Kataleb,* a little above Ainkane, which is also used by the initiates of the Druse Djebel who come either temporarily or to live there as *samnyasin.* They are usually fairly simple, wholesome people who aspire to sanctity. This liberal Druse mentality corresponds fairly well to the evolution of all contemporary societies where ritual seems to be falling into disuse. Rather than religion, it is our social relations, our mores and our culture which link us to one another and distinguish us from the non-Druses. This shared sense of community and morality has more in common with nationalism and a rather vague sense of nationhood than with religious sectarianism.

One can always tell a Druse, by his bearing and manners. The Druses are alert and lively but they behave with great dignity and courtesy in society. They are polite and use special words to express their emotions or to articulate their thoughts. They speak Arabic better than most, and much better than the Christians who do not pronounce the hard consonants. This Druse way of speaking comes from the genuinely Arab roots of all except a few families who came from the Maghreb or Anatolia. The Druses are more discreet, with a sense of the social, the familial and the communal, for all that they are very independent. Even their faces are different. If there is one Druse in a crowd of 20, it will always be easy to pick him out. Passing time has not changed our race, for custom forbids the Druses to marry outside their community: there were few exceptions to this rule.

The language is full of proverbs, expressions and polite turns of phrase which are specific to the Druse. Under the Mandate, Mr. Bart, France's Delegate-General to Mount Lebanon, produced a collection of these sayings. A few examples: 'May God allow me to reward you'; *'Alim Allah',* which means 'God knows men's hearts', 'God knows whether one speaks the truth'; *'Allah yerham bayack aou emmak'* ('May God look down upon your mother and father'); *'Kif hallack ala al fadl'* ('How are you, in your goodness towards us'). The Druses have a keen sense of honour and never forget a service rendered them. That is why they are called *Ben Maarouf,* those who remember the good that has been done them. They will remind you of a good deed you have done ten or even 30 years ago.

A great Druse figure has little concern for his image: appearances are only appearances after all. It is said of the great Fakhriddinne emirs that they were born Druses, lived as Christians and died as Muslims. This is not the case with me. Naturally, I know the Gospels, better than most Christian monks, and quote from them often, but that does not mean that I could ever think of belonging to this or that Christian sect. In any case, I loathe the idea of being tied to any closed society, religious or otherwise. I believe man is of the race of God. He must seek the essence of the Truth through religions, but he must also transcend them. This is the typical Druse way of thought, neither narrow nor formalistic, liberal in spirit and free of all messianism. There is no use in proposing to someone that they become a Druse. Everybody remains what they are. After death, a Druse soul moves on to one Druse body and then another and so on until the end of time.

But a Druse is not only what is usually meant by the term, namely a member of a sect which can be found in Lebanon, in the Djebel in Syria, in Israel, in Turkey or even in North Pakistan: a Druse is a unitarian, somebody who believes in the unity of all the religions of the world, whether the rite be Christian or Buddhist, Muslim or Hindu. Rather like the Rosicrucians, who have adepts in every religion and who in fact claim to be the 'Druses of the West'. There are indeed strange similarities between their beliefs and ours, notably the Rosicrucian devotion to Pythagoras and their belief in the transmigration of souls. But the Druse conception of metempsychosis is slightly different: we believe that after death the soul immediately settles in the body of a baby being born and that it penetrates the flesh through the intake of breath. In its mother's womb, the child had lived only vegetatively: only when the infant begins to breathe does the soul take up residence. The Rosicrucians, on the other hand, believe that the soul may remain for some time in an ethereal or larval state before moving on to another body, and they hold that there is a period of latency between death and rebirth.

In passing, I might mention that I once met an extraordinary young man, a South Lebanese Christian. He would remain wrapped in thought for hours, like someone who had lost himself. One day he came to see me and said: 'Listen, I cannot go on. I am haunted by my previous life; every morning when I wake, it takes me an hour or two to convince myself that I am living another life different from that which I once lived. I am constantly harassed by my past life which hounds me incessantly with its confused images.' He could recall his life in the Munich of over a century ago. He visited the city and recognized his old house, his tomb, everything which had once been familiar to him.

The true Druse faith is the gnostic wisdom of Greece, Egypt, Persia and Islam all in one. It is the 'focus' of all the religions, to use Ruyer's phrase: taken separately, they are only the reverse of the Truth.

One of our problems is the existence of a Druse community in Israel. They are not, as has been claimed, loyal servants of the Jewish state. But the Druses are wise enough not to quit the field when the invader arrives. They are too attached to their land, to the seat of their community. Why flee? Better stay than leave the place to others. This was the principle the Druses applied in 1947 and 1948 when the Israelis attempted to expel the Arabs.

The Druses are truly rational: they have that 'Greek commonsense' which gives them stability. They have an awareness of passing time, and know that one day everything will change, for nothing remains unaltered under the sun. They think far ahead. In short, they have the virtue of hope, because what really justifies a Druse in his own eyes is the unshakeable optimism of his eternal quest. In this sense, the Druses are Heraclitans: there can be no joy unmixed with grief, no fall which is not followed by an ascent, no trough in the sea without the crest of a wave behind it. Above all, there is no real death, only a change of corporal garb: one changes bodies as one changes shirts. '*Oua la tachafou min Tamzik akmisatikom*' (Do not fear to tear your bodily shirt') says the Book of Wisdom, and it adds, 'Do not fear your enemy, for your fear gives him power over you.'

So the Druses stayed and arranged things so that they would not have too much land taken from them and so that their life amongst the Israelis would be bearable. Personally, I feel that if all the others, the Christians and Muslims, had done the same instead of fleeing, there would have been no Israeli problem because there would not have been this vacuum of 1,200,000 people. Think of an Israel with 1,600,000 Arab, Druse, Christian and Sunni inhabitants . . . . . The Israelis would not have brought in so many Jews from abroad, and the Palestinians would have participated fully in the economic life of the country and, therefore, also in its political life. They would have had a share in government, and would indeed have formed an active and strong minority in the Chamber, amounting effectively to a small majority, given that the Jews are so divided amongst themselves and have, to my knowledge, never been able to form a majority government which was not a ramshackle coalition.

Despite the exodus, Druse patriots have done their duty in Israel, struggling against Jewish settlement both politically and militarily, and participating in all the revolutions in Palestine. Many Druses from here joined in these struggles: there is not a single village in the Chouf which has not lost from four to ten young men in the course of raids in Palestine. A great many Druses are still imprisoned in Israel for their patriotic ideas. Several of the most famous Palestinian poets are Druses: Samial and Kassem for example. The Druses have thus done their duty, perhaps more wisely than others, always waiting to see the eventual outcome. They know it is useless to tilt at windmills.

I am of course aware that some of our opponents accuse certain Druses of collaborating with the Israeli Army. It is true that some of them were dragooned by the Israeli military, but since 1967, most Druses have insisted on dispensation from military service. Since then, there has been constant tension between Israelis and Druses, mainly due to the fact that the Israelis have seized a third of Druse lands, under the pretext that it was mountainous terrain. In some villages they have taken up to half of the most fertile fields. The brother of Sheikh Alel is in prison over there because of the protests the Druses organized against certain particularly offensive Israeli measures.

I think the Druses have their finger on the pulse of all Arab nationalism, which is beginning to make considerable headway. They have always been a minority with no minority feelings, unlike the Maronites — that minority obsessed with their sense of being a minority. As fervent partisans of Arab nationalism, Druses have relentlessly participated in the struggle for over a century and helped in the organization of the first societies for the defence of Arabism and political freedom. Indeed, some of these bodies were led by eminent Druses such as Emir Mohamed Arslan, President of the famous Liberation Committee. Similarly many Druses fought alongside Sheriffs Hussein and Feisal during the rebellion against the Turks. Throughout history, the Druse have always been ready to play their part in every war, every revolution. In 1925 they fought against the French for 2 years; it is thanks to the Druses and other patriotic leaders that the Syrians won their independence. The price in blood was paid more dearly by Druses than by anybody else.

As for the question of Druses in Israel — who are so often slandered by our detractors — I would point out that of the 8,000 Muslims who used to serve in the Israeli armed forces, many were Sunni; strangely the Sunnis here — who are always prompt to criticize the Druses — seem to have forgotten the fact. Their sectarian spirit notices the mote in the eye of others, not the beam in their own. In any case, it is unimportant: Druses have given sufficient proof of their nationalism. They have always preached Arabism, perhaps even before the Sunnis who originally were tied to the Ottoman Sultans by Islam. The Druses, who had no such unreflecting inhibitions, were quick to support Arabism against the Turkish yoke. They have always been loyal to Arabism, and have fought in every battle to defend it. No accusation against them can stand.

Unfortunately, it is a long time since we had any relations with the 30,000 Druses in Israel. In the old days, when Palestine was free, they often came to Moukhtara. They are cut off from us now, but they are guided by an eminent spiritual leader who, at more than 80 years of age, is a fine example of wisdom and prudence. Prudence is another of the distinguishing traits of the Druses. They do not shout into the wind; ever alert, they gauge their surroundings and choose their words carefully, assessing what must be said and what can be said.

Notes

1. Governor.
2. Priests.
3. Mystical ecstasy.

3. The Maronite Challenge

'Violence is usually the handmaiden of deceit.'

One of the deep underlying causes of this crisis lies in the strange hiatus which diverted the course of Lebanese history in 1864. On that fateful day, the old Lebanon, which had been committed to an Anglo-Saxon form of liberalism, was torn apart and put to death. As I have already mentioned, this old Lebanon had been dominated by the princes and chieftains of the great Druse families who ruled liberally and rationally. They had needed a great deal of patience to do so: in a way they were the Protestants or the Quakers of Islam. Those days are past. Today, numbers are more important than quality. We are a democracy, the majority decides. The Druses, having become a minority following the emigration of many of them to Syria or the Druse Djebel, and especially after the massacres of 1585, could no longer lay claim to the dominant role that they had historically played in the affairs of the country.

The Petit-Liban invented and maintained by Europe in 1864 survived till 1914, when the Ottomans occupied the Mountain and thus put an end to the semi-autonomy the country had enjoyed. During this historical hiatus, the Christians, or to be more precise, the Maronites, grew used to the exercise of a certain authority over the regional administration. They dominated this Petit-Liban, but only up to a point, since the Druses were well represented on the administrative council. This 50 year parenthesis provided the Maronites with a freshly acquired set of historical memories and created in them a new desire to run the country on a permanent basis. They thus equipped themselves with the structures of a political community, whereas previously they had been content to remain a religious community whose political ambitions were always kept in check. The French Mandate both shaped and consolidated these political aspirations, by conferring upon the Maronites the authority they had never exercised before, either directly or indirectly. In the past, the Maronites had been good scribes, authors, historians and poets, as well as workers, traders and labourers, but they had never been more than that. The Mandate handed them complete political power on a plate, a free gift that they did not deserve, as they themselves have demonstrated. Druses have a saying: Maronites make poor governors, for they lack both the feeling and the tradition of government (the Turks were of the same opinion).

No one can truly govern if they are narrow-minded, self-interested and inclined to deceit, to act in one way and seek something else, to say one thing and do another. These flaws soon disfigured the administration of the Grand-Liban of 1922. The Maronites had not forgotten the Petit-Liban of yesterday, and continued to manifest their sectarian, confessional spirit within the new government. The Maronite community's political education and sense of identity were thus profoundly, one might say definitively marked by the period of the French Mandate, which gave the isolationists — as we have called them ever since — a sense of success comparable to that of the Israelis in Palestine under British Mandate, and later, when they declared a State of their own.

As far as we are concerned, the isolationists are those who seek to isolate Lebanon, to cut it off morally, politically, socially and perhaps even nationally, from the Arab world; those who believe that only a Christian, or rather Maronite, Lebanese nationality exists. This Maronite nationalism, as the historian Hitti calls it, was one day or another bound to come into conflict with an Arab nationalism legitimized by the history of the country, a nationalism which is a blend of Lebanese patriotism and Arabism. During the Mandate, the isolationists entrenched themselves in sectarianism: they were the spoilt children of the colonizers. For them, France was 'our beloved mother'; naturally enough, since it was the institutions of the Mandate which enabled them to exercise that spirit of political segregationism which characterizes them to this day. Democracy had been restricted, notably by the division of seats within the Lebanese Chamber of Deputies, which gave the Christians five Deputies for every four Muslim Deputies. A little later, shortly before 1943, there were five Muslim seats for every six Christian seats. At present, the Christians hold 11 more seats in the Chamber than all the Muslims put together.

This system has never corresponded to any genuine demographic repartition. Just after the Mandate was instituted, the Christians, feeling themselves to be a minority, secured French assent to bolster their numbers by calling in the Armenians who had been pushed out of Turkey. Later, they turned to the Assyrian and Chaldean Christians. But much to the dismay of the isolationists, the Armenians have refused to take part in this fratricidal war we have just been through; their attitude has remained truly liberal and patriotic. They showed that their own Armenian nationalism was fully compatible with their loyalty to Lebanon. They are a fine people, enterprising and very organized. In fact their spirit of enterprise is beginning to worry certain Maronites, especially as they are very prolific. In Beirut, they own about one shop in every five and control most medium-sized industries. No Armenian has ever been seen begging. Nor has any Druse so abased himself. A Druse who is destitute will claim his rights, but he will not beg.

The Constitution that was imposed upon us included an electoral system which gave political predominance to the Maronites; even in terms of the division of seats amongst Christians, they took the lion's share. The Grand-Liban was quite simply created *for* the Maronites. The French made no attempt to hide the fact, and the Maronites proclaimed to all and sundry that 'Had we not been here, there would not have been a Lebanon independent of Syria'. Historically, Lebanon was indeed part of a certain Syrian framework, a natural Syria, which was itself one element within the overall Arab framework. In those days even Sheikh Pierre Gemayel's father gave his address as 'Bikfaya, Syria' on his visiting cards. And letters to us were sent to 'Moukhtara, Syria'. Community sectarianism was a poison transfused by the Maronites into the body of the Grand-Liban from the moment it was born. This sickness may have been tolerable in the homogeneous Petit-Liban of 1864, but it became a festering sore in 1922.

A State cannot be organized on the basis of such an inequitable division into castes, or around a religious spirit which is not shared by the other communities involved. A minority caste enjoyed the privileges of a majority. Throughout the history of Lebanon, many other groups have gone through this unconscious process of transformation from a cultural community into a political community. We are a mosaic of all the religious tendencies, sects and philosophies which have emerged from the various schisms and heresies, be they Christian, Byzantine or Islamic. The Lebanese State officially recognizes 16 distinct communities, but many others exist in our country, the Alawites for example — and new ones are constantly appearing: Dahichism and Jehovah's Witnesses, Ismaelis and Baha'is (that little 19th Century sect which now has over a million followers in the United States).

Unlike in the West, this plethora of creeds has always had an intense cultural coloration. Hellenism, Persian culture, all the ancient civilizations are intertwined here. This is where Islam encountered Byzantium, Egypt, Phoenicia, Iraq, Iran and Greek Hellenism, be it directly or through the Christians of Byzantium and Palestine. Would Jesus himself have existed had it not been for the Hebraic Hellenism of the Romans? What would Muhammad have been, without Abrahamic culture and the impact of Iran?

The Maronites themselves derive from the Aramaic culture which prevailed in Palestine when Jesus was born. They have preserved the ritual Aramaic language in its more evolved Syriac form, and their music, with the specific tonality of its chants, reflects this fact.

Drusism is another example of a religion/culture, derived from and historically prolonging the whole Graeco-Egyptian synthesis, complete with its Iranian contributions. Hamza Ibn Ali, the 'Saint Paul' and main apostle of the new Druse cycle, was Iranian. Drusism is actually Egyptianized Hellenism, but each of the sect's key figures had an Iranian at his side. It is very odd: Jesus had his three wise men, and Sleman el Farsi — the venerated saint of Drusism and Shia Islam who accompanied Muhammad — was of Iranian descent.

As for the religion of Byzantium, it represents the heritage of Byzantine culture, with its pomp, its liberalism and its imperial spirit. The Greek Orthodox and the Greek Catholics, two branches of a single cultural stem, have not been infected with Maronite-Aramaic fanaticism, that virulent microbe nourished by the proximity of Israel, which itself is another form of racial state based on religious nationalism. The Maronites, as inheritors of Aramaic, are much more closely related to the Palestinians they fight than they realize.

Let us complete the picture. Shia Islam is a form of Irano-Muslim protestantism: its capital, the Vatican of its culture, is Najaf el-Sharif in Iraq, not far from Iran, the Shia state *par excellence.* Sunni Islam, on the other hand, is in a way the orthodoxy of the Bedouin, of the man of the desert, who stands historically and typologically naked before his God, Allah. It reflects the Absolute and flourishes in an egalitarian, democratic, semi-patriarchal society, uniting individualism with a sense of community and the cosmic spirit embodied in the notion of the Dar-el-Salaam, the land of Islam forever and everywhere. It involves a monolithism and a gregariousness difficult for a non-Muslim to understand, above all Sunni Islam is the *Shari'a*, the letter of the law. The Sunnis form a very rich cultural community, as is evident in the historical wealth of their rituals, and especially in Sufism. Here, Islam is a world of archetypes and vision.

Lebanon is thus a country characterized by the widest possible cultural diversity, and it would be immensely rich if it came to recognize itself as such. It could have set an example to the world by being the homeland of cultural syncretism and thereby providing a much needed and truly human symbol. We could have given a new meaning to human cohabitation and provided human society with a living example of a different kind of collectivity, an assembly of cultures rather than the Western assembly of individuals, in short, a little 'league of nations'. The Arab-Islamic Empire of yesterday used to fulfil this role by uniting people and races from different cultures and who spoke different languages: the result was an extraordinary cultural renaissance. There are still over two million manuscripts from that period which are yet to be published; an even greater number was destroyed during the Mongol, Tartar and Crusader invasions, when huge libraries and monuments were burnt down. The Lebanese formula could have been ideal, if only people had been content with this symbiosis of heart and spirit within a united and traditionally humane nation, this variety within a unity which went beyond multiplicity.

Can such a dream come true in today's world? Can one really say that the modern state is a humane structure? People speak of modernity as if it were an ideal, some lost Eden. We need to rethink the modern State. Many of our problems stem from a misinterpretation of Rousseau's egalitarianism, from a frantic individualism which cuts people off from their cultural or religious roots in the province or the village. In a similar vein, General de Gaulle also wished for a return to regionalism, to save what could still be saved of provincial or village entities. He knew what to keep from the old days. The village, where everything is on a human scale, contributes a specific ethnic entity. Can a State which lacks such specifications be truly viable in human terms? Can one live in it, honestly? Does it allow one to breathe?

Lebanon's cardinal sin was thus the sectarian spirit introduced by the Maronites who contributed to the destruction of a politico-cultural formula with its multivalent commitment. The impact of Westernization may make it difficult to promote and maintain this distinctive aspect of our country . . . . A half-baked Westernization – and then a simplistic, pragmatic, imperialist and amoral Americanism – have swept over us and over all the peoples of the Third World. We should have liked to find a way of surviving this barbarian invasion of technocracy.

For a while, the Maronites were able to adapt themselves to Arabism. They showed themselves to be particularly enterprising, as most Arabs can testify. They contributed considerably to the development of administration in several Arab countries, and helped promote culture, journalism and the liberal professions. They are good seconds but poor leaders, because they are too attached to their personal interests, to lucre and luxury. They lack the ancient austerity of the monk: perhaps this is a historical reaction to the behaviour laid down in the monastic thought of the order of Saint Maron. They have no conception of either the nation or the state . . . money takes precedence over everything in this part of the Levant. This duality of behaviour and thought finds practical expression in constant equivocation. For most Christians, there is a gulf between concept and action, between intention and will. Their whole approach is redolent of Phariseeism and decadent Hebraism. We have lived with this moral deceitfulness for years. Of course, there were always traditional Islamic leaders and a few Christian intellectuals who sought to hide this by proclaiming that Lebanon was a model to the world, that everybody loved and wished each other well, that it was the land of social friendship, true charity and love. There were indeed positive aspects, but on the whole, reality was very different.

People lied to themselves in this country, even about the 1943 National Pact and Lebanon's independence. There was a lie at the root of it all, and violence was bound to ensue; violence is usually born of deceit. A brave and loyal man will not stoop to violence unless he is forced to defend himself. The ferocity which ravaged Lebanon carried echoes of the practices of some of the ancient Hebrews, when, guided by their God, Yahweh, they swept into Palestine, killing men, women, children, horses, mules and donkeys, burning the harvests, cutting down trees and razing their enemies' houses. Nothing was to be left standing before this barbarian wave, this Bedouin fury, this bandit raid.

What has happened now is in a way a repetition of the sectarianism and nomadism of long ago: further proof that the Maronites are more Arab by descent than they realize. The psychological archetype of the horde still lurked within the modern and civilized Lebanese. This syndrome of violence and rapacity became even more open and apparent due to the moral alienation of the masses, especially amongst the young who were particularly prone to the tensions and psychoses created and reinforced by modern civilization.

Furthermore, the Maronites believed that the Constitution was sacrosant, rather like the Mosaic Law. (Look what they have made of Christianity.) This rejection of any political evolution was the basic material cause of the crisis. To refuse any democratic evolution of the political institutions was to refuse to live with others; it amounted to a rejection of that spirit of compromise and accommodation which is indispensable in social relations. Morally, this Maronite refusal of any genuine evolution was a kind of refusal of both God and humanity.

Another factor in what has just happened was the fact that the dominant political and oligarchic class, the Christians, wanted to maintain Lebanon's character as a 'place of refuge' and opposed any evolution which would have made it possible to bring the Lebanese together in a single nation, as *a people in their own right*. There was a profound antagonism between the 'market-stall' concept of the Middle East and the aspirations of the citizens, especially the young, to have *a real nation of their own*. The choice was between nationhood and the shopkeeper mentality. Yet none of this can justify the bloodbath that ensued.

Our leaders had long been vaunting the Lebanese formula at the four corners of the earth. But this formula was, it seems, just one more myth about our country. If so, it was a particularly well established lie; some societies are built upon a social lie in this way. With time, through much propaganda, it gains a certain power, the power of established fact if not the power of truth. In Lebanon, this precarious adhesion around a lie was doomed eventually to dissolve and disappear, precisely because of the sectarianism in which the religious communities were increasingly entrenched.

Is this tendency specific to the East? It certainly once existed in the West, with the Byzantine sects, the Protestants and the Cathars, but that period of Europe's history is now past. Here, alas, people still cling to it, probably because of a certain lag in moral evolution, because Islam itself has not evolved, and retains, deep in its soul, a Saracen complex *vis-a-vis* the Christians, a neurotic rejection of all that is not Muslim. Of course, the Koran itself recognizes the Christians as believers in the Holy Book, who should thus be treated as equals. But unfortunately, certain interpretations, notably by Ibn Taymiya and various imams who ignored the true spiritual thrust of Islam, saw fit to anathemize all other religions and even a few Muslim sects. Complexes of this kind survived for a long time also within the Catholic Church and in Protestant thinking: for instance, until recently the Vatican considered that several Christian denominations were not truly Christian.

Nonetheless, the French Revolution of 1789, the subsequent separation of Church and State and the promulgation of Napoleon's Civil Code had beneficial consequences and forced a more liberal evolution. Philosophy, too, made a considerable contribution to the practice of political liberalism. Unfortunately Islam has not been fertile ground for philosophers. Avicenna, Averroes and all those who once advanced Islamic thought, eventually withdrew into themselves, stifled by orthodoxy, and have had little influence on present-day Islamic attitudes. Unlike in the West, the orthodoxy of the Muslim East offers no truly philosophical body of thought which could dominate the collective mind. This is a serious lacunae: philosophy has, throughout history, had a crucial influence on people's attitudes and behaviour, as is apparent in the evolution of Ancient Egypt, Greece, India and China.

For all its problems, Lebanon did go through a relatively long period of peace, simply because, with the setting up of the Petit-Liban in 1864, the communities concerned managed to share power more or less fairly, despite the obstacles they faced. A sort of *modus vivendi* existed between the Druses and the Maronites, allowing the Druses to maintain their very relative predominance, but only just. Above all, the head of the executive, the *Moutassarref* of Mount Lebanon, was a Turk nominated by the Sublime Porte and drawn from the ranks of one or other of the small non-Maronite Christian communities, usually the Greek or Armenian Catholics. As a nominee of the Porte, he enjoyed the support of the European six power protectorate which guaranteed Lebanon's new status and a fair balance of power between its citizens.

But this experience of a peace that constantly had to be preserved on an *ad hoc* basis did little to cleanse people's souls. The Maronites were still prisoners of their inexhaustible desire to expand their domains and extend their influence; they shut themselves in through their own fear of being surrounded. In many ways, Zionism is a similar phenomenon; or, at least, the results are comparable: there can be no coexistence in the Maronite State, dominated as it is by a racially exclusive and hence totalitarian orientation. Like the Jewish Zionists, the great majority of Maronites have adopted an imperialist, racialist and confessionalist approach. But the Zionist Jews have had so much contact with European thought, they have kept their traditions and even certain aspects of their traditional mysticism alive, they have, with exceptions, lived more or less freely in Europe and have thus adapted their attitudes. They lack the intensely sick sectarianism of the Maronites. The Jews have committed no excesses *vis-a-vis* the Arabs in any way comparable to what the Maronite isolationists have done to Muslims. The psychotic and mediaeval Maronite mentality is a puzzle which demands careful study.

The Lebanese constitutional structures were so much in contradiction with the principles of an egalitarian and democratic state that the confessionalist status quo was bound to break down one day and drag the whole country with it into a bloody quagmire. Indeed, the very notion of Lebanon as a separate little State was itself an oddity. Throughout history, the country had managed to survive as a small Arab-orientated principality, fulfilling an equivalent role to that of Montenegro. But just like Montenegro, it seemed destined to disappear into a larger natural formation defined by what I would call the natural boundaries of Syria. The carve-up of Syria between the French and the British in 1919 was a fairly barbarous act, and the confessionally based Lebanese formation it spawned was doomed from birth. Let us not forget that in the reign of the semi-independent Lebanese emirs of yesteryear, the country was one element within a Syrian framework and acted as a major force promoting secularization and independence for Syria as a whole. Addressing a conference in 1919, just before General Gouraud announced the creation of the Grand Liban, Father Lamens, the historian, had warned his audience: 'Be careful, do not divide Syria, it is like Christ's shirt, woven from a single thread of linen. To cut it up is to run the risk of destroying it and losing it altogether.' He was referring to the British and the French, who were already sharing out the Levant between them. 'You want Syria,' he continued 'well, then let one of you take it, but take it all! Do not break it up.'

The eventual partition of Syria was indeed purely artificial. Mandate Palestine, Mandate Lebanon, Mandate Syria and Jordan should all have been a single State. Within such a framework, all the minorities could have finally overcome the temptations of sectarianism and committed themselves to that Syro-Arab nationalism which had been the basis for independence struggles throughout the previous 1,200 years. As I see it, this nationalism was the only viable one for the region. People have cobbled together a Lebanese nationalism, a Palestinian nationalism, a Syrian nationalism and a Jordanian nationalism, whilst in fact the whole notion is anti-national and runs counter to the political orientation of our entire history. Historians do not deal in the history of Lebanon, they write the history of Syria, which encompasses the little history of Lebanon. Only a secular, progressive Lebanon freed of confessionalism could ever hope to survive. Confessional Lebanon was doomed from the start. It is only our attachment to democracy — and perhaps the beauty of our country — that makes us hesitate about accepting some formula for Syrian unity. Freedom is, after all, man's dignity.

To be honest, it has to be admitted that we in the Islamic countries have known periods of regression, characterized by the strict and literal enforcement of the *Shari'a*, the Koranic law. These reactionary upsurges are still manifest in more than one Arab country, where civil law concerning criminality and the status of individuals has no real force: the *lex talionis* still applies. This urge to prolong the past, to maintain outdated institutions and to enforce the rulings of Islam considered as both State and religion, this restrictive degeneration of the way the laws are interpreted, has meant that the Christians of Lebanon always felt a bit threatened. But they exaggerated their danger. Conformists, opportunists, insincere clerics or mendacious laymen amongst them deliberately took advantage of the situation to engender a psychosis based on fear.

And yet, the Christians held all the trump cards which would have enabled them to act as true innovators in Lebanon. They are excellent propagandists, and have produced novelists, poets and historians of very great repute: Gibran, Hovemy, Rihani, Fokhoury and Hitti, to name but a few. They could, indeed they should, have been the instigators of a new Renaissance through the introduction into Lebanon of the best the West has to offer in terms of rational evolution and Greek permanence, the philosophy of the Socratic dialogue and of humane liberalism, in short, the existentialism of a new age.

The West I speak of is forever inseparable from Greece; I mean the true West, not that which now trails along behind the high capitalism of the United States. The Christians could have done so much. They could have taught the Arab world Europe's rationality, the thought of the Renaissance, the various philosophies of being and behaviour: they would thus have contributed greatly to the undermining of all the myths and to the spiritual development of their neighbours. Even more, they could have sought to make the Muslims of today aware of Islam's rich heritage as a great civilizing force. The task would have been arduous, but oh, how fruitful for the next generation.

Instead of undertaking this noble mission, Maronite isolationism retracted like an amoeba that has collided with something: it refused to act within its own field of action, the field of action of all Christianity in Lebanon, namely Arabism. The task of propagating Western thought, the task of advancing the rebirth of the immensely rich and humane Arab heritage, the task of regeneration is the duty of all Lebanese, Christian and Muslim alike, wherever they have migrated. Unfortunately, the Maronites turned their backs upon this responsibility: their blindly sectarian adherence to a myth possessed them completely. In the end, it was sect against sect; confrontation was inevitable.

Of course, the war also had economic and social causes. The country had lived too long on foggy liberalism, without laws or frontiers, without moral or human constraints, rather like the Tangiers of yesterday or the Hong Kong of today. It was a kingdom ruled by a mad, grasping and greedy Lebanese mercantilism — the spirit of the Phoenicians. Everybody did what they could to get rich, solely for its own sake and by any available means, including the most arbitrary and immoral. As a result, the old morality crumbled; a morality which had until recently been alive and manifest in people's behaviour; a morality of honest dealing, a little mediaeval, perhaps, but with a sense of what a fair price, a fair wage and a fair reward really mean. Land speculation did the rest. In the old days, there were standard prices. That is over and done with. The morality of the past has been wrecked. Only a few traces of it remain, in the mountain villages.

This illicit money-grabbing degenerated into generalized corruption. The great and wealthy all had their arrangements with the emirs, sheikhs and financial magnates of Kuwait, Saudi Arabia and the Gulf. It was not unusual to see this or that Lebanese millionaire standing for hours, waiting at the airport to welcome a sheikh and pay court to him. Money buys slaves to money.

This wealth that poured into Lebanon — like the gold and precious metals of the Incas which once poured into Europe — created a society that, economically and socially, was monstrously unjust, for all its almost American dynamism. 4% of the population retained 60% of the country's Gross National Income; 96% of the people had to make do with the 40% that remained. There were so many scandals ... Luxurious villas, palaces, springing up from the earth as if by magic, the life-style, the way the rich ate and amused themselves, it all scandalized the ordinary people and the new generation. Money was everything. The distinction between theft and legitimate gain vanished. We were living the apogee of the hundred families, the hundred very rich families, amongst the richest in the Middle East. An enormous gulf separated the simple workman or agricultural labourer, earning between L£7 and L£10 a day, from the financier or businessmen, who might pocket up to L£30,000 in a single afternoon.

Furthermore, these people, who were rolling in money, paid no taxes. Given the general corruption of the administration, they could always find a way. In fact, the administration was their thing, subject to their desire, like the Parliament and the State. They exercised enormous political power, both in the Chamber and in Government, and they did so quite directly. To all intents and purposes, it was they who elected the President of the Republic. Few elections were exceptions to this rule. The oligarchy was in power. President Chehab called it 'the wall of money'. It was thus no problem for them to draft the legislation which enabled them to avoid paying tax.

Meanwhile, the ordinary citizen endured constant harassment. Rents were horribly high and almost completely uncontrolled. The poor suffered terribly. 30 to 50% of the average worker's wage had to go on rent. This is how Beirut's 'poverty belt' developed. People poured into it, living on almost nothing, at the margins of society. There is a good example of one of these shanty towns, at Nabaa, which fell into the hands of the Falangist 'heroes'; or one can go to La Quarantaine to Shyah, to Bourj-Baranjne, etc. There were 16 'poverty zones' within Beirut itself, with no sewers, no electricity, often no drinking water . . . . It looked like 19th Century Europe. State capital and economic aid were never directed towards investment of the kind that provides work for people on a large scale, in agriculture or industry. It was only after a very hard struggle that a Ministry of Industry was set up at all: if a few merchants had not invested in certain factories, the project to establish a general Council of Industry would never have been passed. We were completely at the mercy of the merchants and financiers. Land prices soared and plummeted disgracefully. A small plot of land was more expensive in Beirut than on the Champs Elysees. Nobody gave any thought to the life of the ordinary people. President Chehab made some efforts in this direction but was unable to carry them through. However, he did lay down the basis for a social policy; towards the end of his six-year term,[1] he warned: 'If the rich continue to maintain their privileges at everybody else's expense in this way, there will be a social revolution in Lebanon.' We have just lived through that revolution, which was both democratic and social. It would have been a worthwhile task accomplished, if only Syria had left us the time and the means to carry through what we had started.

No general picture of this kind can be complete without adding that clerical feudalism succeeded in retaining its position throughout. In certain areas, the Church owns a third or one half of all the land (*cazas*), notably in Kesruan, Jbeil and Batran. It is said that 20% of all agricultural land in Lebanon belongs to the clergy. The 'red monk', Father Lebret, who has studied Lebanon's social problem used to say: 'For each monk, one has to reckon a million Lebanese pounds-worth of assets.' Prices have gone up since then, and there are fewer monks: each shaven-headed churchman is now worth between L£10 and L£15 million. The clergy, notably the Bishops and Patriarchs, own vast estates of immense value. They have never agreed to sell them, despite repeated appeals from the Pope, who used to order them to do so and use the money to do good works. One might say that the shaven-headed clerics of Lebanon have halos of gold.

The big estates, especially those of the Maronite clergy, remain a major problem in Lebanon. But the feudalism of the Church, of God's sword, is not the only one. There are also the vast domains of the landlords of the Bekaa Plain and of Akkar. In the Bekaa more than half the available land belongs to five families. On top of which, these lords in their manors enjoy certain privileges and rights over their tenants which are positively mediaeval. In Akkar, the big landlords, and sometimes the priests, levy quite unjustifiable impositions on the ordinary folk who serve them: there have been several rebellions as a result.

One should also mention the estates of the building societies which appropriate the land of the small and middle-level farmers. Under the Mandate, France irrigated nearly 5,000 hectares between Tyre and Saida, but here, too, the peasants and local landowners have now been displaced by the big merchants of Beirut and the land speculators. The little groves of orange and banana trees have disappeared. This geo-political situation was undoubtedly one of the main causes of the socio-political revolution which developed in Lebanon. Again, only the military intervention of our neighbours prevented us from attaining our legitimate aim and putting an end to this scandal.

Speculation was particularly easy, given that the lands concerned, in the mountains and elsewhere, were not particularly profitable, as the ordinary people lacked the financial means to exploit them fully. There is no effective agricultural credit bank in Lebanon. People sold their birthright for immediate profit only. In the mountains, in the Bekaa and Akkar, there are still some very large villages, but all the surrounding land belongs to the Beirut plutocrats. Furthermore, one has to take into account the land owned or acquired directly by the bishoprics, monasteries and so-called charities in Beirut itself, in its suburbs, and in the mountains, as well as their holdings in the finance companies and certain industries (the cement industry, for example). Yet the monks are rather inept speculators, probably because they spend too much time on politics. Also, they tend to concentrate on their own comforts, on fine food and drink, and on playing at being little village barons rather than on doing any genuinely socially useful works. To tell the truth, most of the clergy used to be rather ignorant. In the past, peasants frequently became monks, since in those days those who entered holy orders were allowed to marry: monastic life was thus no great trial. Obviously, this meant that the priests were very close to their flock, and it was natural that they should participate in secular life. That is perhaps the distinguishing feature of the Oriental clergy: the monks here concern themselves far more with Lebanese affairs than with spiritual matters and the hereafter . . . . Of course, a priest was usually sure of a good life . . . .

Another cause of conflict was the emergence in Lebanon of new ideas, notably the Socialist, Marxist, Guevarist and Maoist ideologies. Good intentions and vast quantities of nonsense intermingled. Dozens of study groups were formed by young people, attracted by the glitter of something new. Huge numbers of students contributed to this intellectual upsurge: in all, there were 60,000 in the five universities, an enormous number for a town like Beirut. The Palestinian revolution provided the yeast for this fermentation: everywhere one went, people were talking about the revolution, all day long. The natural idealism of youth did the rest.

Revolution was in fashion, revolt was in the air, everybody wanted change. The right were in an awkward position, especially Mr. Pierre Gemayel and his comrades. They realized that their young people were slipping away from them. So they introduced fascism into the schools, reactivated it within bourgeois Christian society, in an effort to prevent the new progressive ideas from gaining in influence. They used a military framework to contain all these youngsters who aspired to and demanded change, and who were constantly clashing with Parliament, the Constitution and the ruling oligarchy's inefficient and corrupt administration. The intelligentsia continued to spread new ideas, and the split between public opinion and the State grew steadily wider. These ideas spread so quickly; they were actively propagated by many university professors, teachers and officials. Everybody contributed to the moral climate of revolution; a new 'historic bloc' was coming into the world.

Unfortunately, the eventual revolt did not come at the most opportune moment. It began badly, fortuitously, abruptly sparked off by incidents with the Palestinians. It would have been better if this political and social revolution had had two or three more years in which to ripen and then had eventually emerged on the model of the great European revolutions. Because of this premature start religious and sectarian phenomena in Lebanon intermingled with properly ideological mechanisms. Good plants intertwined with rank weeds. The positive ideological influences included that of the repentant Church of John XXIII and Pope Paul VI. Father Teilhard de Chardin's influence was also significant — certain Lebanese intellectuals had read his works, printed on a duplicator, as early as 1936. Many priests, monks and bishops had rallied to the idea of change and preached the 'New Church'. Even some of the sons of the wealthy dreamed of the Gospels, of Marxism, or of Teilhard, and sought a new order in life, thereby perpetuating the dialectic of contradiction between generations and the traditional conflict between fathers and sons described in the 14th Century by the great Arab geo-politician and philosopher, Ibn Khaldun. Even amongst the rich financiers, certain true Christians were lucid and farseeing enough to reject the old order. A handful of priests and bishops actively and successfully encouraged a dissent amongst their followers. However heterogeneous, the spirit of revolt was spreading, a new class was demanding a new age.

Certain priests went so far as to preach the destruction of the existing ecclesiastical structure, so that a new, more evangelical, more popular, more

dynamic Church might emerge, a Church more faithful to the principles of
the old Church of Antioch. One of the most interesting proposals was for a
kind of Islamic-Christian synthesis. In Batrun, one priest started his Masses
with *Allah ou Akhbar* (God is great) or *Bi ism Allah rahman al-rahim* (In
the name of merciful God), both of which are Islamic formulas. In Saint
George's Church in Beirut a leading scholar and professor at the Sorbonne
gave sermons on Muslim mysticism. He preached an end to sectarianism, the
fusion of the 13 or 14 different Christian sects which exist in the Middle
East into one single ecumenical presence, and a return to what he called the
philosophical thought elaborated by the ancient University of Antioch, where
a pan-Oriental catholic thought had once been developed, although, alas,
subsequently forgotten. This idea, close in tenor to that of the Alexandrian
School, which grew out of the harmonious encounter between Greek and
Christian thought, as well as other rational conceptions and even certain
forms of Islamic mysticism, had profoundly marked the Druses and the
Ismaelis. Appeals for such a return to the sources, be they Christian or
Graeco-Oriental, were not new, but they were now very much in keeping with
the spirit of the times and certainly corresponded to a profoundly felt need
amongst Lebanese Christians.

I have already mentioned the clash between generations, a phenomenon
which is even more marked in Europe. Children today are far less attached
to the traditions than their parents. They get a different education at school
and nowadays are conditioned by television and cinema from the moment
they reach the age when such media can begin to shape attitudes. These new
generations are thus even more inclined to break away from the family, to
react against what it represents and to be less inhibited by social or religious
taboos. It will not be long before a similar reaction takes place in the Eastern
Bloc. It is beginning already, but in a sense opposite to what is happening in
the West. Over there, it takes the form of a rejection of insipid materialism
and a renaissance of the old Russian mysticism, as can be seen from the
renewed interest in psychology and para-psychology and in the quest for
an explanation of the origins of matter and the physical world. Marx may
have been correct in most respects, but he no longer provides all the ans-
wers: the gnostic revival continues. Man does not live by bread alone: when
his belly is full, his soul demands attention. In both the Soviet Union and
Eastern Europe, the young, the intellectuals, the clerks, the workers and even
the *apparatchiks* themselves are reacting against a poorly understood
historical materialism. Soviet Marxism looks more and more like a tradition.

In our countries people are reacting against tradition and want something
new, even if it has no other redeeming feature. This revolt of the young
people is quite natural: it corresponds to a historical law which must increasingly be taken into account. Plato refers to it, but the tiny rift of his day
has now become an uncrossable gulf. In our country at least, the young
people's reaction was too flagrant not to attract some riposte from the conservatives, whose ultras started increasingly turning their own movement
towards fascism, spreading panic throughout the political scene and arming

themselves.

This brings us to another cause of the conflagration of 1975. Ever since 1967, the Lebanese right had been stockpiling weapons. The right, more confessional than social in orientation, believed that, following the Arabs' defeat by Israel, they faced a unique opportunity to implement the old project of an exclusively Maronite homeland, a Lebanon isolated from its natural environment – the Arab world – and to tighten their links with the West, America and Israel to the point of becoming vassals of these powers. It was then, as we saw earlier, that the main Maronite Church and lay leaders gathered around ex-presidents Shamun and Helou and said, in effect: 'The Arabs are beaten and will not pick themselves up for a good while. Here is our ideal opportunity, if only we wake up to it, to try and impose our Maronite policy once and for all.'

It was around this time that Shamun began to organize his infamous *Noumours*, his 'Tigers'. Everybody here remembers how he solemnly paraded them through the streets that year (1967) in Saadiyatr, after a meeting of the leaders of political Maronitism. The Falangists also set about completing their arsenal. By 1968-69 they were almost ready; in 1970-72, they had 6,000 to 8,000 men under arms. It was clear to everybody that they were preparing for war, and tension rose sharply. There were too many guns in the hands of the reactionaries: this race to arms was bound to lead to an explosion, and the danger polarized around the Palestinians. There had to be a victim, somebody on whom to try out all those weapons. The fanatics started spreading rumours that there were a million Palestinians here, and that they were in the process of carving out a little national State for themselves within Lebanon. It was suggested that they intended to appropriate the south of the country for themselves, that they had decided to settle there because they knew they could never go back to Israel. Bad news is always listened to attentively, and any secret which is leaked soon takes on the dimensions of a myth.

On 13 April 1975, the bloody incident at Ain Remanneh – 27 Palestinians massacred by the Christian Militias – triggered the inferno. It was only then that the left, the Muslims, and patriots of every shade began to arm themselves seriously. It was too late!

Events in Lebanon cannot be separated from the general Middle Eastern context. Without the war in Sinai and the defeat in the Golan, such a confrontation would probably not have taken place. And the Israelis were by no means innocent bystanders in this affair. Their plan was to promote the formation of small, more or less independent, confessional and nationalist States around Israel, the Jewish State: for instance a Druse State, an Alawite State, a Maronite State, a Kurdish State, etc. This plan was drawn up before Israel was established, but only publicly formulated afterwards. Various texts outline these intentions, for instance the official letters between Prime Minister Sharett and his Ambassador in Rome, which talk about the proposed sub-division of the area into little confessional mini-states, thereby allowing Israel to survive as the dominant regional power. The head of

Israel's Foreign Ministry in fact confirmed this desire to see a Maronite entity established. Israel would then no longer be surrounded by Arab states. The Israelis were thus deeply involved in the Lebanese War, along with their patron, the United States. Kissinger is even supposed to have said: 'To content Syria and turn her attention away from the Golan, give her a part of Lebanon.' It may be that it is precisely this plan which was put into effect.

The Americans, as everybody knows, have little concern for principle; their own interests always take precedence. Perhaps Syria stupidly allowed herself to be tricked into furthering such an Israeli-American plan . . . . Or perhaps it was mere bad judgement; one should not underestimate the egocentrism, the irrationality and the ambition of Syria's Ba'athist leaders. They often lurch uncomprehendingly into the purely contingent, for fear of the future, out of an illusionary and ill-defined sense of their interests, or out of short-sighted concern for immediate advantage. There is little room for principle in all this. The Syrians are inclined to look at things in the short term only. Were they deliberately invited to intervene in our country, or — to repeat — did they just fall into an American-Israeli trap? History will eventually provide the answer; it often happens that once in power, left-wing parties unconsciously implement right-wing policies in order to retain their position. Versatile or vacillating politicians are particularly prone to this psychological tendency. Many communist leaders display similar traits in foreign policy matters.

One should also remember the attraction exercised by the long cherished project of a 'Greater Syria'. Furthermore, it has to be said that the Arab world as a whole had watched jealously as Lebanon developed into one of the richest States in the region, yet somehow managed to retain its democratic liberties. In a sense, Lebanon was the victim of the latent jealousy of its neighbours.

Not content with having played a major role in triggering off the Lebanese conflagration, Israel subsequently began to supply arms in great quantities to Shamun and the Falangists. In fact, the military aid provided to the Lebanese right by the United States often comes via Israel. Furthermore, the sea off Lebanon's south coast was regularly patrolled by Israeli coast-guard vessels which took care to ensure that no arms or munitions should get through to the Lebanese National Movement. The Israelis had a very special interest in seeing Lebanon destroyed and what it stood for obliterated; in the eyes of the world, our country was the polar opposite of the Zionist prototype. The Lebanese State was living proof that several communities could live and work together in peace. Its destruction was thus expected to provide some justification for the Israelis' sectarianism and their refusal to allow the return of the Palestinian Muslims and Christians they had expelled. For Israel, the idea of a racially homogeneous State based on the isolationism of the Jewish community is paramount. Once again, Lebanon provided an awkward counterpoint.

The Maronite fanatics fell into the Israeli trap all the more easily, in that propaganda against the Lebanese left was widely disseminated throughout the Arab world and even elsewhere. Everybody was busily hounding a hypothetical Lebanese communism, thereby completely neglecting the real problem. Indeed this wilful blindness even affected governments like that of Syria, in which communists play a role, albeit only a token one. They all exhibited a consummate artistry in manipulating what was happening in Lebanon. Yet the Communist Party in Lebanon, a country based on service industries, is as yet a relatively uninfluential political entity, still sincerely searching for a way to insert itself into the Lebanese and Arab context. Israel acted with tremendous skill, dexterity and caution, and Kissinger evinced the same genius for manipulation. As for the Europeans, they sat back and watched prudishly, although some States allowed themselves to be drawn into the plot.

Marx once said, 'We know the role stupidity has played in history and how it has been exploited by rascals.' If all active politicians — be they socialist, communist or something else — were truly aware of this fact, they would surely be infinitely more modest. If Cleopatra's nose had been shorter . . . .

It has to be said that the Palestinians themselves, by violating Lebanese law, bearing arms as they chose and policing certain important points of access to the capital, actually furthered the plot that had been hatched against them. They carelessly exposed themselves to criticism and even to hatred. High officials and administrators were occasionally stopped and asked for their identity papers by Palestinian patrols. From time to time, Lebanese citizens and foreigners were arrested and imprisoned, on the true or false pretext of having posed a threat to the Palestinian revolution. Such actions were, at first, forgiven, but became increasingly difficult to tolerate. Outsiders making the law in Lebanon, armed demonstrations and ceremonies, military funerals for martyrs of the revolution, it all mounted up and began to alienate public opinion, especially conservative opinion, which was particularly concerned about security. Industry and commerce, the main activities of the Christians and especially of the Maronites, required a stable society. I never saw a less discreet, less cautious revolution. If the Palestinians had implemented the rules I had suggested to them when I was Minister of the Interior, they would never have fallen into this trap.

But in any case, the isolationists had aspired to a Maronite State ever since Emir Fakhreddinne II brought them into Lebanon three centuries ago. There are strange parallels with Zionism here. A Maronite diaspora gradually spread throughout the world, and from the middle of the 19th Century began to develop a communal political consciousness. The creation of the Petit-Liban in 1864 encouraged them to pursue their politico-religious adventure, and, in the meantime, the diaspora westernized and enriched them. In the two Americas, they created a form of Arab literature with its own specific coloration but which, strangely enough, usually contradicted their political aspirations, as the work of Madi, Gibran, Farhat and Nouemy amply illustrates.

Nonetheless, exile did not change them very deeply. It is said that a

Lebanese who emigrates takes three things with him to which he will cling as though they were a family heirloom: firstly, his concern with his personal dignity (*wajaha*), in other words everything that can give him a little bourgeois prestige; secondly, the accent of his village, which he will retain even in Spanish or in English; thirdly, his parochial fanaticism. One might add three other elements: the hollowed-out stone in which *kebbe* is prepared — the Lebanese like to eat well; a cult of self-interest; and a taste for malicious gossip. Many a Lebanese emigrant returned almost totally unchanged, exactly the same person as the one who had left 30 or 50 years before. Any changes were only on the surface, indeed they had often not even kept up with the evolution of their homeland.

The Maronites, in particular, are a living example of a specific collective unconscious, the *eyregore* of the theosophists, which for centuries has been coagulating around the theme of the emancipation of the Maronite personality, and which expresses itself as the creation and intensification of the collective *karma* of the community. Westernization has shaped their attitudes but has not altered the depths of their souls. Perhaps this shows that men are neither free nor masters of their own destiny; they are the playthings of their subjectivity, that psychological 'cassette' which is specific to them alone, which indelibly stamps its imprint upon their individual and collective behaviour, and which expresses the structure of their mental archetype.

At one time, the Maronites were impregnated with European culture, and assimilated it so assiduously that by the 18th Century they were widely reputed for their intellectual gifts. In Italy, 'as learned as a Maronite' was a common compliment. Their conversation was reputed to revolve constantly around points of scientific or philosophical interest. Yet it seems that this intellectualism corrupted more than it elevated them, and helped to make them even more fanatical. They were seen as good clerics, as good tillers of the earth, as able in all things and as endowed with an ability to innovate. Hence their feelings of superiority *vis-a-vis* the non-Christians who were generally less enterprising and slower in their responses. Furthermore, the Maronites managed to preserve the links established amongst themselves by their clerical elite. The influence of the monks was and still is considerable, in both secular and religious matters. They identified themselves with the destiny of their 'nation' rather like the Old Testament Levites did *vis-a-vis* the Jews. One of my Maronite friends, who directs a convent, used to stress the important role played in the community by the monasteries.

Unlike in the West, a Maronite monk remains close to his flock, indeed he is its leader. In the East the boundaries between the religious and the political, the private and the public are always vague and indistinct. As in Islam, the notion of the Patriarch is crucial, just like in the days of Abraham and Moses. The monks have always been both spiritual and political leaders; they never withdraw from the secular arena. They are the standard-bearers of fundamentalist Maronitism and the cement which binds the diaspora together. I was not joking when I compared them to the Levites of ancient

Israel; in the last analysis, one can say of the Maronites that they have been the people of Saint Maron, just as one can say that the Jews are the people of David or of Jehovah. The existence of a people often rests on the myths that surround a historical personality; Saint Maron is one such myth. *'Allah mnih, bass chou bi jibo la Mar Maroun'* says the Maronite proverb: 'God is good, but who can be compared to Saint Maron?'

The Maronites thus constitute a separate entity in their mountain and in their valleys. (In Lebanon, valleys have played an important role in the formation of communities; the Kadishah Valley in the case of the Maronites, the Wadi el-Taim Valley for the Druses). They were alert to culture but never really evolved; they remained ambivalent, open and closed at the same time. There is a dichotomy in their character and behaviour which explains why their sudden upsurges of religious fervour alternate with bouts of extreme nationalism, such as the one we are witnessing today. This fundamental paradox of the Maronite personality helps us to understand why they say one thing and do another. Two personalities co-exist within them, and the result is psychosis. Cruel and benevolent, understanding and obtuse, charitable and ferocious, sincere and hypocritical, that is the Maronites. It was, after all, a Maronite, Mr. Raymond Edde, who invented — or rediscovered — the Arabic term *izdiwajiye* (duality) as a way of describing the behaviour of certain Lebanese politicians.

The Maronites thus dreamt of a national structure of their own, an association psychologically derived from the semi-tribal groupings of early Christianity, an entity based in a little homeland where they could, as they put it, feel free in their own way. It is always the most intensely conditioned people who tend to speak most of freedom, that is a constant of human nature. The existence of such conditioning is particularly revealing of the deep underlying temperament of men, of the mechanisms of sects, ideologies, religions, parties or societies. Man is, in the end, very unfree: he is almost programmed. This explains why all these 'peoples' living together in Lebanon were so different from one another and could not understand each other. It is this kind of conditioning which leads individuals into religious, communal and even racial fanaticism, and which precipitated the Maronites into such ferocity.

The phenomenon is not new; in fact, it is no doubt merely a repetition of the events of the previous century. One should not conclude that the other Lebanese communities lack this destructive chauvinism, but it is most marked amongst the Maronites. The Maronites were the first 'Zionists' of the Arab Middle East. Indeed they were more committed to the idea than the Jews who, despite their millenarian dreams, tolerated divergences and accepted pluralism; there are so many Jewish sects . . . some even go so far as to condemn the existence of the Jewish State. The school of esoteric wisdom known as the Kabala situates its philosophy beyond notions of the terrestial or even the heavenly kingdom. There is, in the Jewish consciousness, a 'detachment from mundane history which has characterized the Jewish people's remarkable contribution to the march of ideas and which has enabled them to retain a sense of the human and the cosmic: And the spirit of God moved upon the waters.' This Jewish awareness of permanence is noticeable in their music, in what they have given the world in terms of philosophy and art, and even in their behaviour in Israel. Until now, practically no *fedayeen* prisoners have ever been executed; by contrast, most of the supposedly progressive Arab regimes have liquidated dozens or even hundreds of people, often without any real trial. As for the Maronites, over time many of them seem to have completely forgotten the real meaning of Christianity.

In any case, few Maronites are practising Christians to any great extent and their relations with Rome are rather vague, sometimes even conflicting: in short, they are 'legalized heretics'. Probably fewer than 50% of the Maronites go to church. Maronitism is primarily an ethnic, mental, communal bond, with a quasi-feudal character. One is this or that lord's liegeman with greater devotion than ever in the Middle Ages in France, for he is the symbol of the collective soul. From this point of view, the Maronites live in the past, they are 'fossils from before the age of modern civilization' as Mr. Dean Brown, President Ford's emissary to Lebanon, once put it. He went on to add: 'Their brains are prehistoric, fossilized . . . . ' The average Maronite goes to church only to get married — since, in Lebanon, the law insists on a religious marriage. He will only return in his coffin — propriety requires a church funeral. Yet despite their lack of religiosity, the Maronites are attached to their saints, their monks and their priests, even if they sometimes hate them and often criticize them. In Maronite eyes, the clergy symbolize duration, continuity: it is they who perpetuate this anachronistic sect right in the middle of the 20th Century.

Not surprisingly, the Maronite Bishops and Patriarchs bitterly contested the new teachings of Popes John XXIII and Paul VI. I well remember the famous quarrel I had with a venerable Patriarch, an old friend of mine, who refused to publish John XXIII's encyclicals in Arabic, especially the one concerning 'The Church as Mother'. He thought that John XXIII was a socialist — or worse, that he was a rebel and was doing a disservice to the Church. This attachment to tradition is manifest in the liturgical Mass, which is still said in Syriac (a development of Aramaic, the language of Jesus) and has barely changed in more than a thousand years. More recently, however, the priests have finally realized that practically nobody understood Syriac any more and that people were praying in an unknown language, which constituted a real rift between God and the faithful. Despite their reticence, they were eventually forced to abandon Syriac in favour of Arabic for normal services. Certain ancient rhythms and the old Syriac music have also been readapted, but the tradition is preserved in the splendid costumes of the Bishops and Patriarchs, in the colours, the rings, the gold crosses . . . all so reminiscent of Byzantium. Jesus, of course, never thought of wearing golden rings on his fingers. But the few monks and priests who sought to do away with this conformism by adopting a costume different from that of the counts and paladins of the Middle Ages were soon called to order. Indeed, one of our good friends, the old Greek Catholic Archbishop of Beirut, a deeply Christian and generous man, was considered as a renegade by many Maronites. Yet the path he followed was one of simplicity and charity: he had abolished the custom by which bishops and priests were richly remunerated for their Masses. This measure aroused such hostility, even within his own denomination, that he was stripped of the Archbishopric of Beirut on the grounds of theological deviation.

Most clerics of the Maronite Church seem to be completely blind to the needs of the country's social and economic evolution. However, in recent years, under the pressure of events, there has been a tendency towards greater flexibility: the present Patriarch, and many bishops, are opting for a reform of the Church and a return to the sources, in an effort to move closer to Jesus's practice. But, as a result, they are beginning to lose influence and it is thus the political prelates such as Mr. Shamun, or the sincere lunatics such as Pierre Gemayel, whose authority over the Maronite 'nation' is growing, since it is they who are more in tune with the isolationist spirit and its propensity to reject everything which seems new or which has anything to do with social equality or redistributive justice. From this angle, Maronitism is the closed society *par excellence*, like the Hebraic society of the bad old days; a community which is more biblical than evangelical. Whoever commits himself to the Zion of this low earth, with its luxury, its pomp and its privileges, denies the Zion of Heaven.

Perhaps it is because of this terrestrial fanaticism that the Maronites are so active and enterprising. They are extremely resourceful and always manage to come out on top. In Arabic, we say that they are *chuter*, which means skilful: in fact, they value cunning more than intelligence. In short, they are true Phoenicians, in the bad sense of the word — they have the ability to adapt to every situation and to fit in with the caprices of all the mighty of the earth. The moment it is a question of business, no sacrifice of their personal dignity is too great, they will prostrate themselves before a client and kiss his hands. If only that were all! But there is worse: a few do not hesitate to line their pockets by providing young Lebanese to certain pernicious sheikhs from the Gulf. They unashamedly engage in the white slave trade. Lucre and greed rule. They are pastmasters when it comes to playing on the rapacious sensibilities of the magnates, and they swindle almost everybody they deal with, especially in the Arab world, where they poke their noses into every deal involving some sheikh, potentate or emir.

Obviously, I am only referring to a certain Maronite *haute bourgeoisie*. The community is not entirely made up of rascals. Many — perhaps a third — are true patriots, courageous, sincere, honest, uncompromising and excellent friends to have. This section of Maronitism has played an important role in Lebanon over the last three centuries, especially in the renaissance of Arab literature during the 18th and 19th Centuries, as well as in the creation of the press, the introduction of printing and the development of administration and Arab nationalism both in Lebanon and in the neighbouring region. Boustany and Rihani are fitting symbols of this open-minded spirit today.

By contrast, the isolationists are now more sectarian than ever. They still hold their secret high council, where clerics and laymen gather each week to analyse the political situation and people's behaviour. The propaganda elaborated in this political and religious Sanhedrin is broadcast very effectively by the press, the radio and especially by the organization's own telegraph network. Word of mouth also works wonders, and is endlessly stimulated by priests, monks and laymen. News and orders spread like wildfire. Whether it be in Saudi Arabia, in Libya, in Brazil, in Canada, Australia or the United States, wherever the Maronites have emigrated to, they all drag along the same old prejudices, the same interpretation of events, the same version of the facts, the same fears. They are thus programmed like automata, conditioned like sleepwalkers, all blindly adopting the same ideas and the same approach simultaneously. Their diplomats and their emigrant organizations are the willing accomplices of this generalized manipulation.

But obviously, as the number of people taking monastic or priestly orders falls, the influence of the Maronite Sanhedrin can be expected to decline. New ideas must eventually make some headway. And now, there is the Syrian 'big stick' to worry about.

Enough commentaries. The following 'charter' of this Zionized nation is more eloquent than any number of analyses. Everybody should know that, just like the ancient Hebrews, the Maronites have received their own Ten Commandments. The only difference is that the author of these Commandments is not God but Mammon (a truly Phoenician inheritance); they are far more down to earth than spiritual. The Charter was discovered in 1920, in a convent high up in the Metn. I do not know who left it there; some workmen found it, quite by accident. It is an address, a message 'from the motherland to her faithful children' and has been attributed to the France of yesterday, the 'beloved mother' of the Maronite people. It faithfully reflects a tradition which has lasted for centuries, ever since the Maronites established themselves in Lebanon, but which remains very influential, especially as the isolationists apply it to the letter.

Oh, sons of Jesus Christ, you who have been educated in his teachings over the ages, who have suffered malevolence and oppression for centuries in defence of your beliefs, Oh noble and pure ones, never forget these ten commandments:

(1) This homeland was created for you alone, that you should gather here and exercise your freedom after the historic wars [probably a reference to the fratricidal religious wars of 1841-60]. Know that the word Lebanese means Christian [that is to say Maronite]. As for the Arabs, they came out of the desert and must return there [Arab means Muslim in the text].
(2) We have so arranged matters that you be guaranteed an honest and comfortable life in this part of the world. Amongst other things, we have made it easy for you to appropriate the land of the infidels.
In the 18th and 19th Centuries, the Vatican and other European

States provided financial assistance to help the Maronites monopolize representation within the international agencies, political status and everything connected with money.] We have put all this in your hands: all you have to do is keep what you have won and make it prosper over time.

(3) Strive to take control of every aspect of tourism, holiday-making and the beaches, and gradually expel anybody who is not one of you from your villages. Become an overwhelming majority in the village. Do not forget to build a port to replace Beirut, a port where there are no Muslims, as soon as you can. [That was the port of Jounie, and more recently, the airport at Hamat, near Batrun.]

(4) Retain all the instruments of power, such as physical sport, weapons, youth organizations. Take care of the army and ensure that it is *your* army. At all times achieve your ends and carry out your tasks in complete secret, albeit while maintaining trust amongst yourselves; the struggle against the enemy, the Muslim, will be long and constant, for they surround you on all sides. [The true spirit of the Crusades.]

(5) Take care always to be in the forefront of literature. Keep a hold over the trade unions and professional bodies. Never allow it to be said that the heritage of your language and history belong only to Islam. Fight remorselessly against any ideas or individuals standing in the way of your activities.

(6) Any divergences that arise amongst you, the Christians, must never go beyond the superficial or the theoretical, because your whole life must be mortgaged to your union against the infidel enemy. Remember that you are the children of Jesus, who taught us all charity. [sic]

(7) Always study the opponent's plan, penetrate his most secret councils and learn about everything he is preparing. You will always be able to find some amongst you who can pretend to join the enemy whenever it proves necessary. But each and every one of you must at all times be linked to his superiors and his Church, and never disobey the orders of the sincere fathers in your ranks.

(8) Lift your heads up high and raise your banners everywhere. Carry out your rituals on every hill and mountain, in all the high places. Remember that all the powerful forces of the free world are behind you and are ready to stand by you immediately. But you must nonetheless behave as if you did not know it.

(9) Try to ingratiate yourselves with Arab Kings and Presidents, by means of medical and personal services rendered. That should be simple enough for you and it will open up vast and varied fields of activity to you, and prove most lucrative and will assure you of considerable influence, even in countries which seemingly reject you.

(10) The battle for Lebanese nationality is vital. You must always be able to control very closely the process by which foreigners are naturalized. Always take good care of your emigrant brothers and of those who come into your country from neighbouring regions; strive

to preserve your rights as a majority, that majority we have won for you. Without that, all your efforts will be in vain.

(Author's interpolations in square brackets)

This document was probably drawn up by monks and laymen gathered in some sort of secret conclave. To this day, as I said, the Maronites continue to meet once or twice a week to decide upon their approach to certain important questions. These decisions are then broadcast to the world through the monks, the bishops, certain laymen and various organizations; the procedure is not unlike that of the Freemasons. This method has always been applied with meticulous care. They are now up in arms against the press, because it has been subsidized by the Arab countries and is increasingly escaping Maronite control, especially the newspapers belonging to the political parties. They want to have a law passed restricting their freedom. Above all, they would like to ban all foreign subsidies, even though when, in my capacity as a Minister, I proposed doing precisely that, they rejected the idea.

These secret meetings first began shortly after the arrival of Napoleon I in the Middle East. Recently this conclave, now promoted to the rank of an 'institution', has taken the name of the Maronite University in which it meets: the Kaslik. It is from there that they carry on their 'research' and publish carefully edited 'political studies' aimed at their flock, who are generally kept in the dark about the underlying strategic design. It is more than likely, for instance, that only the great amongst the Maronites know of the existence of the Charter of the Ten Commandments. I myself saw it for the first time only in 1944. I have heard it mentioned vaguely in the past, but it is only recently that I have discovered the extent to which that document has oriented the course of Christian isolationism and defined their methods. Clearly, most Christians have implemented its precepts, consciously or unconsciously, given that the Maronite leaders succeeded long ago in transforming all the other Christian communities into satellites.

However, the backing mentioned in the Charter is obviously no longer available. France now takes only a distant and rather theoretical interest in what is known as 'the Maronite nation'. She is more concerned to see a united Lebanon, in which the Christians can and must occupy a particular position. This is why, during the recent events, the Maronites constantly raged against France — and against the Vatican, another traditional patron — neither of whom, to our knowledge, supplied them with funds or weapons. Nowadays, they rely far more on Israel, the enemy of the Arabs and their natural ally in the region; furthermore, they are counting on the possibility that the new American administration will look upon them favourably. Strangely enough, they also hope that by raising the spectre of communism, they will be able to blackmail many Arab states into backing them. The Arab leaders, preoccupied as they are with the pleasures of this world, all too frequently see no further than the end of their noses. As the Prophet puts it, 'wealth has corrupted them'. The isolationists, zealous parasites of the Arab Gulf States, are excellent purveyors of hedonistic opium and pastmasters in the art of drawing profit from the internecine conflicts which have cost the Arabs so dear. It is because of the Arabs' inability to get on with each other that they lost Palestine and allowed the Israelis to triumph.

Having said all this, one must recognize that there are many independent thinkers amongst the Maronites, men who refuse to be blinded by sectarianism and overwhelming chauvinism. But alas, as I have said, they form only a third or less of the Maronite world. Even so, they manage to live in the present rather than the past, to keep up-to-date with new attitudes and ideas, and to look upon the future objectively. They have oriented, and in many cases even led, all the national and social struggles of our country. They have been members of all the socially liberal and patriotic movements. This courageous and enlightened section of the Maronite population has never enjoyed the support or encouragement of the State or the political leaders (in any case, the electoral law favours only the isolationists) — or of most of the traditional leaders of Lebanese Islam, the majority of whom have shown themselves to be stupid, narrow-minded, petty and without any real understanding of history. Deserted by everybody, this Maronite elite continues to struggle and resist, and has at times singlehandedly introduced vital reforms. Only the nationalist, socialist or simply moderately left-wing parties have sought to form an alliance with them. These 'true Maronites', these true Christians, are the *fedayeen* of the Lebanese and Arab patriotic movement. It is from the ranks of these men of goodwill that the leaders of Arab liberalism in Lebanon have been drawn, men such as Amun Zakkur, Bechara el-Khoury, the Takla Greek Catholics, etc., as well as the true partisans of Lebanese integrity such as Edde, Khazen, the Protestant Ayub Tabet and so many others.

As for the rest, the traditionalist, Levitic and excessively grasping wing of the Maronites, I would call them a Christian nation devoid of the Christian virtue of hope. They are haunted by the overpowering fear which permeates the soul of deviationist and traditionalist Maronitism. Boulas, an intelligent, cultured and honest Maronite leader who, like so many other Christians, nonetheless allowed himself to be dragged into the mire of isolationism during the recent events, once illustrated this paranoia when he told me, 'The Maronites are like a flock of sheep who, over the ages, have been put to flight by the clanging of a piece of metal [a reference to the historic vexations inflicted upon the Christians by Islam]. Every time the flock settles down, you only have to come near and strike your little gong for all the sheep to take off again in a panic, pausing a little further on and waiting, terrified, for the next sudden sound.'

This atavistic psychosis has been carefully cultivated, deliberately fuelled and constantly exploited by a clerico-secular clique of fanatics, opportunists and political salesmen.

Notes

1. The Lebanese President is elected for a six-year term.

4. The Palestinian Detonator

'Subconsciously, they reproach them for being poor, stripped
of political rights and robbed of their country.'

Contrary to the isolationists' allegations, the civil war would have broken
out even without the presence of the Palestinians. Lebanon needed no such
pretext to become the scene of bloody confrontation in 1958. The
Palestinian resistance was only *one* cause of the latest conflict. If the
Lebanese had not been ready for an explosion, there would have been no
explosion. The truth is that the Palestinian presence — and especially their
numbers, which rose from 110,000 in 1948 to over 400,000 in 1975 —
did frighten the Maronites. They feared that in 10 or 15 years the number
of Palestinian refugees would have swollen to over a million, and that internal
troubles would ensue, since with the 500,000 Syrians and other Arabs living
in Lebanon, there would, according to them, be far too many foreigners in
the country. The Palestinian presence thus exacerbated the Maronites'
anxieties.

Unfortunately, they failed to understand that nothing could be done
about it and that the problem called for a quite different approach, based on
appeals to their contacts throughout the world. They could have explained
to their American, European and other friends that the only way of solving
the Palestinian issue was to reintegrate the 1,200,000 Palestinians — including
those in Lebanon, of course — into Israel, in other words to implement the
1947 U.N. resolutions. Rather than embarking on a 'crusade', the Maronites
would have done better to call on the several million individuals of Lebanese
origin living abroad, and on various influential Europeans, to take an interest
in finding a real solution to the Palestinian problem. Instead, they underestimated the military forces aligned against them, notably that of the
Palestinians, and chose to cross swords. They thought that the Army would
march with them, but as it turned out, the Army only followed them up to
a point and eventually fell apart. So we are now back to where we started,
and, as far as the isolationists are concerned, the situation has worsened; on
a military level, the Palestinians are now even more powerful than before,
despite the chastening presence of the Syrians, and they enjoy what I will
call the protection of the Arab Summit, which was granted them at Riyadh

and Cairo. Above all, Arab opinion on the subject is more sensitive than ever, a fact that will inevitably find popular expression sooner rather than later.

Nonetheless, from now on the Palestinians will have to conform to the Cairo Agreements[1] more strictly than before, especially as these agreements give them a great deal of political manoeuvring space and considerable freedom to organize. The day will come, in the not too distant future, when the Palestinians will have to proclaim a provisional government and organize themselves differently, with their militias becoming an 'allied army' stationed in Lebanon, as part of the preparations for a Geneva Conference. The Cairo Agreements could easily have been implemented through the joint efforts of a good Minister of the Interior and Palestinian officials sincerely committed to a policy of co-operation.

The Palestinians wanted help in organizing themselves. But how could the Lebanese have responded to this need when they themselves were totally disorganized? To create the proper circumstances within which to force the Palestinians to adopt a certain discipline, order must first be established amongst the Lebanese. The Palestinians should entrust the maintenance of order within the camps to the units of the Palestine Liberation Army[2] stationed in Lebanon, rather than to disparate and sometimes competing militias. They should also agree to collaborate in every instance with the Lebanese authorities, so as to ensure that, in future, fugitives from the law should not find sanctuary in the camps. The administrative and police authorities in the camps should allow the Lebanese at least the right of inspection. This in no way implies any encroachment upon the principle of Palestinian sovereignty over the camps, but Palestinian common law criminals should be handed over to the Lebanese State to be judged according to Lebanese law. Measures should also be taken to make the camps more human: administrative and budgetary co-operation between the Palestinian municipalities and the neighbouring Lebanese municipalities could be established so as to ensure a minimum level of sanitation and sewerage.

All this would help the Palestinians to become more organized and orderly. They need to feel that someone is taking an interest in them. Their feeling of being abandoned and treated as pariahs could easily be eliminated; they have, until now, been so misunderstood and illtreated by the Arab regimes. A certain sense of human dignity must be restored to the Palestinians, who at present often live as refugees in ghettoes amongst the Arab population and suffer constant political exploitation by all and sundry, including the supposedly progressive regimes. The Lebanese State should integrate the Palestinians more harmoniously into the active life of the country. The human contacts that would result are indispensable to mutual understanding: the absolutely aberrant relations between Palestinians and Maronites would certainly be improved thereby. The creation of a Ministry of Palestinian Affairs would usefully co-ordinate all these proposals. But first, trust has to be re-established.

Obviously, the Lebanese State is still too weak to undertake these reforms immediately. But one should not lose hope. The State could be restored and security could return, if the administration made up its mind to appoint a good Security Chief, raise the salaries of the police and double their numbers.

However, the problems are not restricted to Lebanon itself. Most of the Arab regimes no longer wish to be told about the Palestinians. They subconsciously reproach them for being poor, stripped of political rights and robbed of their homeland. One of my friends, a Lebanese communist, recently said to me: 'In the West or even elsewhere in the world, when a people are struggling for independence or are suffering heavy discrimination, they are at least supported by their own kin. Here, in the Arab world, they are picked on and doubly victimized instead, as a punishment for disturbing the peace.'

This is, indeed, what is happening on the Arab political chess-board. For the nth time, the Palestinians have been the victims of their ruling Arab compatriots. And yet, the $8-10,000 million paid out to Egypt and Syria by the oil states during each of the last three years would have been amply enough to liberate not one but two Israels. And this sum is nothing to the new barons of the 20th Century. But the rich Arab States do not want to be disturbed; they prefer to allocate their budget to their own development rather than to a war of liberation. Nonetheless, I believe that, in the long run, things will change. As long as a remnant of democracy subsists in Lebanon, the Palestinians will retain their political freedom. (The present censorship of the Lebanese press is unlikely to last for ever.) But it is crucial that the Arab powers stop subsidizing, individually, their own little contingent within the Palestinian revolution. All the subsidies, both guns and money, should be turned over to the P.L.O., the only legitimate representative of the Palestinian people, through the offices of a common fund controlled jointly by the Arab League and the Resistance. This would contribute a great deal to reinforcing the cohesion of the Palestinian Revolution, by considerably reducing the likelihood of antagonisms developing in the future.

The resistance may be composed of the most divergent political tendencies, but Yasser Arafat has always quite openly maintained that the fundamental requirement of liberating the land of Palestine took precedence over any ideological disagreements. Later, everybody will be able to start their own parties and defend their own ideological position. In the meantime, the national cause is paramount. To worry excessively about what one will do with one's liberated homeland, at a time when it is still under occupation, is a clear case of putting the cart before the horse. Naturally, it is necessary to have one's own ideas on the subject, but these should not be the prime concern.

For the moment, Arab nationalism must remain the main ideological support for the struggle against Zionism. Whilst a particular social project may indeed contribute to bringing people together, it can also lead to antagonisms and differences between groups who need to be united to win. We are, let us remember, in the Levant and we have inherited a tradition of Byzantine quarrels; if we are to pursue a national cause to good effect, we must form as broad a front as possible. To each his own opinions, but, as I see it, the Palestinian people cannot yet afford the luxury of committing themselves to socialism or to communism; there would be too many disagreements.

In any case, neither socialism nor communism would have any place in today's world if they were still confined by the disincarnate and dogmatic context which was once theirs. There is an urgent need to return to what I would call the economic, social and political categories that human evolution has revealed, and to make them the basis and criterion of all political philosophy and of every social or economic realization. This implies a spirit of pragmatism linked to change and oriented towards the perennial human values. There is no room either for realism or idealism. We must transcend both terms to discover *relative truth,* which evolves within a changing context and framework, yet is always a manifestation of the immutable, the face of the eternal.

To come back to Yasser Arafat, it has to be said that he was never very popular with the Syrian leaders. The Lebanese affair did nothing to help matters, nor did the co-ordination between the Palestinian Resistance and the Lebanese National Movement. In practice, Arafat frequently followed the advice of our movement. He saw it as a way of freeing himself from the Syrian yoke, which was growing burdensome: control over the sale and movement of arms, reinforcement of the Saika, in fact constant attempts to impose Syrian tutelage.

If they had left him alone, the P.L.O. leader would quite possibly not have provoked the break with the Syrians. But as it was, he was all too aware of the plot that was being hatched against him. So were we. Because of this threat, all our interests were intertwined; Palestinians and Lebanese co-operated actively and a sort of symbiosis and mutual influence developed (except in military matters, in which the Palestinians insisted that everybody dance to their tune). We all felt anxious about the intentions of the Syrians, and eventually had no choice but to break with them when it became apparent that the Syrian plan was geared to draw maximum advantage from the painful circumstances and tragic events in Lebanon. The Palestinians felt that they were as much in the line of fire as the Lebanese. 'Philip of Macedon' and his army were at our gates.

The Syrians wanted to impose themselves and their point of view, their interests, ideas and tutelage, upon everybody. They only appeared to be seeking an equilibrium between the belligerents in order to be able to intervene freely and make the most of the situation for themselves. The Syrian military intervention, following the partial failure of their political arbitration, revealed the Damascus regime's real intentions. At first, the Americans and Israelis had opposed the direct invasion of Lebanon, but they later encouraged the military adventure; no doubt they banked on the Syrian regime's determination to do away with the independence of the P.L.O. and the Lebanese left. Arafat had no choice but to defend himself, and nor did we. Furthermore, Saudi Arabia and Arab reaction in general also egged on the Syrians: they saw the *de facto* co-operation and symbiosis between the Palestinian Revolution and the Lebanese National Movement as a danger which, if left to itself, would inevitably spread. It was a marriage they felt they had to break. Also, anti-communist propaganda was rife. The Arab world establishment — the rich and the powerful — could not tolerate the onslaught of the changes which had been set in motion. Saudi Arabia, for instance, clearly played a part in the hardening of Syrian attitudes, even if they did not turn away from Yasser Arafat, who remained, for everybody, a symbol and a guarantee.

He, at least, cannot be charged with dogmatism, and the relations between us during the war were always good. We are in the same boat; for the Palestinians as for us, the main thing was to weather the storm. But we always remained committed to adopting clear positions and even to preserving a certain relative distance; as we saw it, Lebanese affairs should be a matter only for the Lebanese, which naturally meant that we had our own political battle to fight. We must now continue that struggle, so as to implement the reforms we proposed and which were taken up so enthusiastically by the young people of this country — and perhaps others, since our ideas have spread throughout the Arab world.

The Palestinians, like everybody else, managed to extricate themselves from the Lebanese hornet's nest without any permanent damage. In the final analysis, all of us, including the isolationists, were lucky to survive. The alternative was too dreadful to contemplate: the deathtrap of Syrian totalitarianism, and the loss of all democratic liberties. One can only hope that this tragedy will lead to a serious re-evaluation. The Palestinians must bear it in mind. There must be an end to the anarchy which reigns both within the Resistance and amongst the Lebanese. Had there not been so many breaches of the law, we would not have witnessed such fury against the Palestinians on the part of the isolationists.

Unfortunately, it is not in Israel's interest that things should go well in Lebanon. Given the present climate, the Israelis are likely to take measures of their own. The Jewish State did not believe that the Arab world was capable of reacting quickly and sending in troops to quell the fighting in Lebanon. Obviously, Israel's attitude will depend, in part, on that of the United States. If the latter takes a firm decision to put an end to our problems, if they give the green light to the Arab world, and to Syria in particular, to re-establish order in Lebanon, Israel will probably not be able to do very much — especially as Damascus and Cairo are now on better terms and Jordan too is playing its part. The Arab world is regrouping, perhaps because of what has happened in Lebanon. Israel will have to take this Arab consensus into account. As to the future, it is, as I have often said, vital that Europe should once again seek a role in the Levant and concern itself increasingly with our affairs, so as to enable us to become freer *vis-a-vis* Israel and the two super-powers. The world situation would be considerably improved thereby.

But we are not there yet. 25,000 Syrian troops are still stationed in

Lebanon, a presence which represents a serious latent danger. To what extent will Arab opinion be able to prevent unwarranted interference in the affairs of the Lebanese and Palestinians? There is a conflict between democracy and dictatorship: those who are not free always wish to prevent others from being so. Damascus wants the Palestinians integrated into the Syrian camp. But that will prove to be no easy task — especially once the mirage of Geneva has been dissipated. Will the Syrian regime then not seek to pull back a little, in order to improve its image in the Arab world? The old Lebanon, that democratic chaos, that endless jumble of freedoms, so dear to the political parties, the common people and the Palestinians, will then, at last, have to face up to its responsibilities, reorganize everything and put a little more discipline into Lebanese and Palestinian affairs. Will democracy survive, or will it be strangled, as so many Arab countries would like? One can only hope that the Lebanese will manage to defend their freedom; with European help it should not prove impossible.

As to the Palestinians, the crucial thing is to reach an understanding. They must adopt a clear position — a 'strategic position' as our revolutionary intellectuals put it; in other words, they must define the common ends of their struggle and draw up a short-term plan of action. It seems to me that all Palestinians could agree to a tactical solution based on the complete implementation of the 1947 U.N. resolutions: the return of the 1,200,000 Palestinians to Israel, with full political rights, just like any other citizen, and the formation of a small Palestinian state within the frontiers laid down by the U.N. in 1947, comprising 46% of historical Palestine, in Upper Galilee, Gaza, the West Bank of the Jordan, etc., etc. Having had many long discussions with the various Palestinian organizations, it seems to me that this is the minimum that they could eventually accept. The idea has also been put forward by President Habib Bourguiba; I believe it to be a sound and pragmatic proposal.

I know that neither the U.S., nor Europe, nor Israel, share this viewpoint, but in the end, inevitably, everybody will have to come together on this basis, since we are talking of U.N. resolutions which should be respected by *all* States. They took part in passing these resolutions, they must now seek to implement them, if there is ever to be an end to this conflict.

Notes

1. The Lebanese-Palestinian Agreements of November 1969.
2. The P.L.O.'s regular army.

5. The Syrian Trap

'We threatened to draw them towards a destination they had no
wish to reach, in other words, towards democracy.'

To understand the strategic manoeuvrings of Damascus, one must first take
into account the personal ambitions of the Syrian leaders, the political aims
of President Hafez el-Assad and his projects for a Greater Syria.

Given the ever-present political threat from Iraq, the signature of the Sinai
Agreements by President Sadat left Syria in an over-isolated position. Domes-
tically, too, the regime faced difficulties. It would seem that during the
1975 regional and local elections, only 15% of electors voted, despite the
fact that the polling booths were kept open for two extra days. To obtain
some settlement over the Golan, Damascus was forced to 'go American',
to move closer to the U.S., without, however, distancing itself in any
apparent way from the U.S.S.R. Furthermore, the economy was not healthy,
since the Saudis had considerably reduced their subsidies to major Syrian
projects. During the previous two years, there had been a surprising
rapprochement with King Hussein's Jordan, of whom Damascus used to
speak so ill.

As for the settlement of the Lebanese conflict, the Syrian leaders came
increasingly to treat it as a matter of personal prestige. Syria's diplomatic
successes with Jordan were not enough to re-establish her standing in the
Arab world. There were points to be scored in Lebanon, and Syria sought to
win them. Step by step, what had started out as 'assistance' collapsed into
an insane military intervention. The Syrians should have done as we advised
and contented themselves with acting as arbiters between those factions that
were running wild. For all our warnings of the dangers such a military intervention carried for them, for us and indeed for the whole Arab world, they
carried on regardless. We even warned of the possible Israeli reaction, but to
no avail. Now, Israel is building itself a buffer State in the south to keep the
Syrians at a distance. For the frustrated Ba'athist leadership, it was important
to appear in European and American eyes as the undisputed and influential
leader of this part of the Arab world. The protection granted to the Maronites
seemed a good way to move towards better relations with the West. Lebanon
was reduced to a trump card in Syria's hand, with the restoration of the

Golan Heights as the stakes. But the Americans, and especially the Israelis, played the game very skilfully, banking boldly on Syria's ambitions and on her complex, ambiguous and stubbornly self-interested foreign policy, to drag her increasingly towards interventionism and into the 'swamp', as the Syrian Minister Khaddam aptly described it.

Additionally, like all the Arab governments, Damascus dreaded possible contamination from political democracy in Lebanon. A State which would be both progressive and democratic was the nightmare of all these authoritarian regimes. The prospect terrified them. The truth is always explosive. The Lebanese press was frighteningly free. Furthermore, in an effort to win Saudi Arabian approval, the Syrians made a point of evincing considerable hostility towards the idea of the erection of socialism in Lebanon, picking out the communists — the Saudis' pet hate — for particular vilification. Syrian diplomacy touted this idea to the Arab regimes, in order to convince them of Syria's good intentions and to allay the fears rightly aroused by her federative projects. The over-ambitious intentions laid at our door were grossly exaggerated: we sought only to protect the Palestinian Revolution, which was threatened by the Arab plot, and to institute a fairer and more democratic system in Lebanon.

Historians should also note another element: the spontaneous political attraction between minority blocs — the Ba'athist regime in Syria and the Maronites in Lebanon. The religious and collective unconscious often lurks behind political action.

Alongside the Syrian Ba'ath Party's anxieties as a political minority, a political Alawitism — like that of every other minority and even of Sunni Islam itself, although the reasons are different — incorporated and developed two contradictory tendencies, the one making for isolationism and the other pushing for total Arabization and Arab unity. In Ba'athist Syria these two tendencies balance each other out in a constant battle for power. But the overall popular verdict of political Alawitism gives preference to the Arab unionist current, even if this tendency has to be toned down once power is achieved. This is usually what happens, except when a leader of the political stature of Nasser emerges and upsets the applecart. Normally, however, it is isolationism which prevails in practice, even if under the cover of slogans proclaiming 'Liberty! Socialism! Arab Unity!' Hence the unconscious convergence with isolationism in Lebanon.

The other Alawite political current, which was opposed to the Syrian military intervention, is now taking its revenge by demanding a federation with Lebanon. The elimination of political confessionalism and the establishment of a wider form of democracy in Lebanon could have had far-reaching consequences in Syria and in all the Muslim countries of the Arab world. The fact cannot be avoided; the rulers of Damascus hardly bothered to hide their indulgence *vis-a-vis* the massacres perpetrated by the Maronites. The pretext was the attempt to win them over to the Arab cause, but in reality the aim of the Syrian military intervention was to finally stifle the Palestinians, our own National Movement and the Lebanese left generally.

Not content with seeking to woo the Maronites by a means to which they have always been susceptible, namely the provision of protection (to which they are, of course, all the more susceptible if the protector in question happens to be a Catholic Western state) the Syrian leaders were determined to repress the political movement that was hostile to these same Maronites, or at least to keep a firm rein on both tendencies. Some reflex of self-preservation, quite opposed to any genuine revolutionary aspirations, induced them to preserve the Maronite entity as a dependency of the existing Syrian political entity. The right wing of the Syrian Ba'ath Party was by no means a stranger to this approach, especially as the policy accurately reflected the pragmatic relations between the Syrian regime and certain Lebanese capitalists who were quite willing to provide payment for 'services rendered'. Lebanon's untramelled capitalism was far too good a source of profit to individuals throughout the Arab world for them simply to accept its disappearance. And let us not forget a certain Damascene rapacity or the jealousy aroused by these Lebanese who were obviously so good at enriching themselves. The Saika and its associates were looting Beirut even before the intrusion of the Syrian troops. After all, the great houses of Beirut were practically museums, packed with Louis XIV and Louis XV furniture, Persian and Anatolian carpets and many other treasures from India or Japan. The Lebanese have always had a taste for the grand style. I will pass over the eventual systematic pillage of Beirut and its banks — the nomad seems to have awakened in every breast, including that of a good many Lebanese. Morality is far from what it could be in Lebanon. Hooliganism is all too common amongst the young. The phoney culture which floats in like scum from the West actively encourages these attitudes.

The Syrians also aimed to isolate Sadat's Egypt and make the most of the disappointment so many people had felt when the Sinai Agreements were signed. Also, the Syrians needed some brilliant success in order to appear as Egypt's peer and win a reconciliation. Egypt remains the most influential State in the Arab world, the 'bastion of Arabism'. (Arab speech-making is prone to such cliches.) The country is densely populated and endowed with a vast arsenal of civilian equipment, including both aviation and maritime companies. The Azhar el-Sherif (the Vatican of Islam) is in Egypt, bearing witness to a specific historic continuity. Egypt is the only state which can be seen as an effective base for the liberation of Palestine, given the necessary Syrian-Iraqi alliance. Bear in mind that, looming in the background, there is the ever present image of Gamal Abd el-Nasser, who has become a myth to all the Arab peoples. Egypt, be it Sadat's, Nasser's or that of some other Pharaoh, inspires enormous confidence in all the Arabs, hence the astonishing rapidity of the Syrian-Egyptian reconciliation at Riyadh. The relative stability of its institutions — despite the recent upheavals — has always made Cairo, under the Fatimids or under Nasser, the political pole (*kibli*) towards which the Arab peoples all turn. The Egyptian Army remains a seductive mirage of material and psychological strength. Syria, which has to cope with Israel on its southern borders and Iraqi political pressure to the east, could not, given these conditions and despite many often valid objections to the Sinai Agreements, avoid returning to the Egyptian orbit sooner or later. The Syrian regime's policy of protecting the isolationists in Lebanon could only hasten the rapprochement. Indeed, Egypt and Syria's historical destiny dictates that they should unite, even if only around a shared political line. As Rene Grousset once said, Egypt is really part of the Levant. Syria thus had to score some notable achievement. Unlike in Egypt, where the ruler is usually assured of a long reign, the authorities in Syria cannot maintain their position without winning some minor victory every six or seven months. After all, the country has witnessed some 15 military coups since 1948. The base is always restless, too restless even, and something constantly has to be done to keep people quiet. It has to be admitted, however, that Assad has managed to impose a measure of stability.

Lebanon offered the Syrians the opportunity they needed, the chance to appear as the negotiators *par excellence,* the 'solvers' of the Lebanese problem. President Assad saw himself as the man of the moment. The egocentrism characteristic of so many politicians, especially dictators, is usually an element in such situations. Furthermore, Damascus has always dreamt of Lebanon: hence the privileged relations with President Frangie, the refusal to allow him to resign, the constant support for him. For the Syrian authorities, Frangie was the man who could make a Syrian satellite out of Lebanon. We were amongst the first to detect this ambition, and it was the basis for our early conflicts with Syria. This forced vassalization was quite unacceptable to us. I do not know how King Hussein felt about it either . . . . Perhaps the Syrians had some notion of re-forming Greater Syria even then; who knows?

Nor were the Palestinians absent from the Syrians' preoccupations. Relations between President Assad and the Resistance have not always been as smooth as they might have been. Once the Palestinians had emancipated themselves from Arab tutelage and could no longer be patronized, the Syrian Ba'ath Party, like the other Arab regimes, began to feel bitter about being outshone by the successes of the new command of the Resistance. The Palestinians' position on the international scene was becoming something remarkable, and more than one Arab leader was envious. Harsh words were exchanged between Syrian and Palestinian leaders. It does not take much to remind the Syrians of the past: they sometimes seem to consider themselves the only genuine representatives of Palestine, which as far as they are concerned is simply the southernmost region within Syria's natural boundaries. Furthermore, Syria wanted no new problems on its flanks, and the Arab world had no wish to be shaken out of its lethargy. Almost everywhere, there were people who dreaded the idea of change in Lebanon, the possibility that it might cease to be the pleasure garden so dear to rich and influential Arabs. Others feared that communism might be stowed away somewhere in our baggage train. This argument, widely broadcast by Damascus, was to cause a furore throughout the Middle East. Everybody feared our radicalism and our desire for independence. We were nobody's clients.

Strangely, I got on well with Hafez el-Assad; we respected each other, and I give him full credit for having granted the Syrians a little more freedom. But when he sought to impose his ideas on Lebanon, about which he knew so little, we had to say no! Our Syrian friends wanted to solve the Lebanese problem in their way, from above, artificially, with no genuine development of the constitutional law of a democratic parliamentary regime. They barely remember the concept. Military dictatorship by a minority has made them hostile to all democracy. The 'presidential message' agreed by ex-President Frangie and the Minister of Foreign Affairs proposed a Constitution which was a caricature of parliamentary democracy. Our considered rejection of this supposedly constitutional message proclaimed on 14 February 1976 by Frangie (a complete ignoramus in constitutional matters) must have brought down upon us the displeasure of Minister Khaddam and, eventually, that of the Syrian President himself. As for us, we never acted out of malice. We were simply convinced that we could not accept an irrational and anti-parliamentary Constitution which ran against the fundamental principles of civil liberty.

As I always said to President Assad, 'I enjoy maintaining relations with the Syrian State, but the Ba'ath Party, which as far as I can see is ideologically vacuous and totally devoid of any concern for public opinion, is quite another matter. The Ba'ath may be well intentioned, perhaps even honest, but it is not serious.' No objections were raised when I said this, in fact people agreed; I have never hesitated to speak the truth when the need arose, without malice or ulterior motive. Remember, I only became a politician by accident. . . .

All we had to oppose to this 'Holy Alliance' between totalitarian fundamentalist Maronitism and the Syrians, was our commitment, the inflexible and honest determination of our people. One need not always bend before a passing storm. We remained firm as an oak. Then the Syrians robbed us of our political victory, just as our patriotic militias were occupying the outskirts of Bikfaya and Kesruan. They surrounded us and broke our stride. Alas, as I kept telling President Assad and anybody who would listen, the racist fascism of the Falangists, of Shamun and company, first had to be broken militarily if one was later to deal with it politically and, eventually, heal it psychologically. Let it pass . . . in five or ten years hence, we shall see to whom the final political victory will fall. The Lebanese masses, more conscious and determined than ever before, are already on the move. The main thing is that we feel we have done our duty. We have faced our *karma*.

Apart from the political reasons behind the 'Holy Alliance' between the Syrians and the Maronites, there were other types of interests involved. I will mention only in passing the relations between Frangie and certain figures in the Syrian President's entourage, some of whom were in fact relatives of Boutras el-Khoury, the great Lebanese industrial and finance magnate.

Personal factors played a not insignificant part in this affair, especially the protagonists' own individual characters. For instance, President Assad's personality is a mixture of commonsense, honesty, loyalty to his friends (the Frangies), a sense of balance, stubbornness, skill in manipulating antagonisms and a certain natural benevolence, but there is also duplicity and hardness. The big stick is always in the background and is usually an essential factor in his regime's approach. Apart from the fact that he listens far too much to his four or five different intelligence services, he is a man who knows what he wants and how to get it, by guile if needs be. During his intervention in Lebanon, he showed himself vindictive and compassionate by turns. He seemed moved to pity by the massacres, the destruction and the atrocities of the Lebanese civil war; indeed, he claimed that such sentiments played a large part in his decision to intervene, and to this day, the regime advances this as an argument. By dint of repeating something, one comes to believe it oneself and to act accordingly. Pretexts disguise one's real intentions. Ordinary human nature is complex enough, but when one is dealing with politicians, party leaders or a military junta, life gets even more complicated. Everything is jumbled together: sincerity, ambiguity, ambition, destiny, and above all, the quest for power. On top of which, just as there is always a trace of the Pharaoh in Egyptian rulers, one can always detect the *wali* in Syrian chiefs. It is no easy task to distinguish the good intentions from the bad in such a tangle.

If the truth be told, the Syrian authorities have almost always held an ambivalent position; the Ba'ath Party has never freed itself of its ambiguities. And in the background, there lurked the semi-defeat of the 1973 war; it was not enough to transform it verbally into a victory, it had to be transcended, blotted out altogether. Generally speaking, the Syrians used to be the ultras, the 'young turks' of the Arab and Palestinian cause. It is thus all the more difficult to understand why they should suddenly go back so completely on this traditional nationalist attitude. Especially as a regime devoid of any lucid rational ideology and which disallows all political freedom can claim as its own whatever motives it chooses. But I believe that, personal factors apart, there was a very important political component to the decision; Syria felt isolated. The Saudi and Kuwaiti mandarins' contribution to Syria's military development had become a mediocre trickle. For the past two years [since 1976-7], Syria had been striving to whip up Arab public opinion against the Egyptian initiatives, and the endeavour had not been without cost. Arab opinion was weary of accusations of high treason hurled about indiscriminately, especially as everybody knew that Syria too had sought a compromise, even though, given the present Arab and international context, it could not possibly have been a good compromise.

Prudently, Iraq had said its piece on the Sinai Agreements very frankly, but without having recourse to the kind of personal attacks employed in Damascus. Iraq is known to be opposed to any compromise whatsoever, but it did not break off relations with Egypt for all that. On the contrary, Baghdad reinforced its co-operation with Cairo, in order to restrain what they saw as the Egyptian tendency to swing further and further towards a policy of compromise. In practice, the Sinai Agreements did less damage to the future of the Palestinian cause than the military confrontation with the Syrians.

Let us look at things as they are; the Sinai Agreements proposed a suspension of hostilities and a disengagement, followed in the long term by preparations for peace between Egypt and Israel. The dream of an immediate and total liberation of Palestine was finally dispelled. In fact, most Arab politicians and statesmen no longer envisage such an outcome: that does not prevent them shouting at the top of their voice about it in the public square. The Arabs are still all too prone to this kind of complex selfdeception. The Arab world needs a policy based on principles not on slogans.

Be that as it may; the Sinai Agreements led to serious dissensions amongst the Arabs, especially between Egypt and Syria, Egypt and Libya, etc. Furthermore, Egypt lost a great deal of its political manoeuvring space and freedom of movement in the process; the agreement carried with it a heavy diplomatic liability both on the international and the Arab level. Another unfortunate consequence was the alienation of the Soviet Union, by now bored with carrying this Arab burden which, in the last analysis, brought only debts and very little prestige.

Nonetheless, if one examines the text of the Sinai Agreement itself, one cannot avoid the conclusion that it in no way mortgages the future, and especially not that of the Palestinian people. None of the clauses runs counter to the ultimate aspirations of the Palestinian people, their return to their country, their unity and their right to decide their own fate. The agreement could achieve little because it was signed at a time when Egypt was going through an acute economic crisis and felt itself abandoned by the rich oil States. The Egyptian regime sought only to liberate the Canal and the Abu-Rodeiss oil fields; it needed some concrete achievement to offer the Egyptian people in exchange for their support. The Egyptians are tired of fighting for the Arabs and in the name of the Arabs without ever getting anything in return. Every year they have a million new mouths to feed, a million new people to clothe and provide jobs for. Their massive debt to the Soviet Union weighed heavily upon them, and the oil-rich States were proving almost squalidly miserly. Nor should one forget the endless quarrels between the Arabs, the lack of any sense of solidarity and responsibility, the noisy hyperbole from Damascus and the simple fact that Nasser was no longer there to crack the moral whip. Yet it has to be said that the Sinai Agreements cost Egypt and the Arabs very dear. Israel received $4,000 million dollars in military and economic aid from the Americans, and won surprising guarantees in exchange for withdrawing from the Giddi and Mitla passes, returning the Abu-Rodeiss oil fields and allowing the Suez Canal to be opened once more. But it was the miserliness of the Arabs and their irresponsibility which forced Egypt to sign. Egypt owed $11,000 million to the U.S.S.R. and other creditors: the oil magnates were providing only just enough to stave off the death of thousands of Egyptians, thinking thereby to keep the country on a tight leash. The American logic was very similar.

Looked at closely, it is clear that the Sinai Agreements were far less harmful to the Palestinian Resistance than Syria's systematic aggression, which put the starkest possible choice to the Palestinians: surrender or die. The Syrian regime felt all the more isolated when the other Arab countries refused to follow it in its vituperations against Egypt. Even the pure hard nationalists of Algeria, for all the stern criticisms they directed at the Sinai Agreements, opted for a more cautious and dignified approach.

One should bear in mind that, after Sinai, Mr. Kissinger had not managed to force the Israelis to withdraw from the Golan. Does this shed a different light on the advantages of the Sinai Agreements? Perhaps; in any case, Syria, no longer finding the support it sought from the U.S.S.R., turned its coat and decided to play into the hands of the Americans and impose a police regime in Lebanon.

The regime had opted for a *de facto* alignment with the U.S. By opposing the Lebanese National Movement, the patriotic Christian leaders and the Muslim population in their efforts towards popular liberation, and by launching into confrontation with the P.L.O., the Syrians went much farther than the Egyptians in terms of applying America's containment policy. Two years ago, none of us would have imagined that Syria would embark on a military intrusion so much at odds with her traditional policy. It would seem that Geneva — that impossible dream, the mirage of Geneva — had become an obsession. Having run up against the Israelis' stubborn refusal to cede a single metre of the Golan, especially in the Heights which, as Syrian diplomacy constantly reminds all and sundry, are so crucial to her defences, the Syrians changed tack completely and demanded a comprehensive settlement of the whole Middle East crisis, including the Palestinian problem. They felt that in the upheaval of such all-embracing negotiations, involving the creation of a small Palestinian State on the West Bank of the Jordan, their chances of getting back the Golan were much better.

Another personal factor was that the present Syrian rulers have always detested Yasser Arafat. Even in 1967, when Hafez el-Assad was Minister of Defence and just as the Palestinian Revolution was getting into its stride, having asserted its independence from all the Arab countries, Yasser Arafat and some of his companions were arrested and imprisoned in Syria, near the border with Israel. Was this a preventive measure, a way of avoiding Israeli reactions to Palestinian 'terrorism'? Later, in 1970, during the Amman events,[1] the Syrians, after much procrastination, decided to watch from the sidelines: they even refused to allow the 16 Palestinian battalions stationed on the frontier to go to the rescue of their comrades who were being massacred by the Jordanian artillery. The pretext was the need to avoid the worst, namely an Israeli or American military intervention in Jordan.

President Assad is a tenacious man and quite capable of acting very directly once he makes up his mind, but most of the time he is very cautious, to the point of indecision. Of course, although these views are widespread in certain circles, one should always take what one hears with a pinch of salt; not for nothing are the Arabs, and especially the Levantines, known as the

'People of the Word'. However, a few years back, I myself had to intervene repeatedly to re-establish a degree of understanding between Yasser Arafat and President Assad, in a period when invective was flowing thick and fast out of Damascus; President Assad can be over-sensitive and often reacts according to his feelings.

In any case, the Ba'athists in Damascus believe that the Palestinian Revolution should march hand--in-hand with the Syrian authorities and should even be *represented* by those authorities. Ignoring the present, they refuse to forget the days before the carve-up of 1919, when the Lebanese, the Palestinians, the Jordanians and the Syrians formed a single people, the people of historic Syria, covering the area from the Taurus Mountains to Sinai and from the Iraqi steppes to the sea. Indeed, President Assad confirmed this quite unambiguously to Yasser Arafat not so long ago (around April 1976): 'You do not represent Palestine as much as we do. Never forget this one point; there is no such thing as the Palestinian people, there is no Palestinian entity, there is only Syria! You are an integral part of the Syrian people, Palestine is an integral part of Syria. Therefore it is we, the Syrian authorities, who are the true representatives of the Palestinian people.' On this occasion, at least, the 'Lion of Greater Syria' put his viewpoint frankly enough. In fact, Syrian nationalism has always expressed itself thus in moments of crisis. For the Syrians, this is the starting point of Arab unity. There has been so much talk in Syria of Arab unity, freedom and socialism — the trinity of Ba'athist slogans; strange that nothing has been done to put them into practice.

In terms of freedom, it is undeniably true that people in Syria are a little freer under President Assad than they were in the days of his predecessors. But we are still a long way from the political democracy aspired to by this liberal and rebellious Mediterranean people. The Ba'ath Party, for all that it was highly westernized to begin with, made the mistake of copying the Bolshevik one-party system of so-called popular democracy. Perhaps the fact that it was always in a minority had something to do with it.

As for socialism, apart from the nationalization of most industries and a more or less equitable land reform, it has had no impact whatsoever on the retail trade or on urban property. The ordinary people and minor state employees are severely pressed by rising prices and soaring rents. Against this background, a new class of millionaires has emerged, to the great indignation of the people. Something similar has been taking place in Egypt just recently .... The new policy should have been supplemented by a fixed ceiling for rents at around 8 to 10% of the cost of construction, without taking into account the cost of the land on which the building or apartment stands. Individual ownership of rentable property ought to have been limited to a maximum of one building, and a ceiling set on the income which could be derived from it (say from 50,000 to 70,000 Syrian pounds, for example). This would have been the only way to break the rising spiral of land prices, rationalize rents and block this major source of the general inflation which has swept through Syria, Lebanon, the Arab countries and indeed the whole world. An angry petty bourgeoisie can be very dangerous!

If we now turn to Arab unity, the subject of so many slogans and speeches, the first thing that springs to mind is the break-up of the union with Egypt, for which the badly organized Ba'ath Party of those days was partly responsible. The memory weighs heavily on the Syrian and Ba'athist conscience and on Arab public opinion. No longer is anybody taken in by all the hyperbole about unions which turn out to be purely conjunctural tribal agreements (now with Egypt, now with Jordan). Consequently, the leaders of the Syrian Ba'ath dream of realizing, just for once, a real federal union. But with whom? With Lebanon, where Syrian troops are now stationed in force. This psychological element in present Syrian policy will continue to be a factor, along with the expectation that an eventual confederation with Jordan will — who knows? — result in recovering the Golan.

To sum up, there were two more or less defendable theses concerning the Lebanese problem: the Syrian thesis of a benevolent and humanitarian policing role — at least that was how their military interventionism was presented and justified to the world; and the Lebanese thesis, our thesis, the thesis of the Lebanese National Movement, which, as we see it, is more in keeping with the real interests of Syria itself, of the Arab nation and of Lebanon, and thus more in harmony with a practical revolutionary spirit concerned with effective progress. Unfortunately, in the Arab world, it is often a thankless task to speak in terms of realism and efficacity.

The Syrian approach was rather conformist, indicating a lack of interest in the problems of a people — in this case the Lebanese people — and devoid of even the most timid revolutionary spirit. It was a bourgeois policy, of a kind which prevails — or at least manifests itself — in many socialist countries throughout the world. The Ba'ath Party, like most other Arab political groups, lacks a real sense of dialectic. The Syrian leaders have read neither Socrates nor Heraclitus — their Hellenization has been sadly inadequate. The teachings of the School of Antioch were buried long ago in the ashes of the passing centuries, just like those of the famous School of Alexandria. The break with Hellenism is the cardinal sin of this inverted Semitism. Greek thought survives only in the schools of Sufi Islam. It ought to be more widespread.

By rejecting its Greek inheritance, present-day Islam seems to have regressed, just as early Christianity did in Europe, when the barbarian spirit penetrated the Church and the neophytes turned to a spirit of negation and destruction. The 'Turkicization' of yesterday still dominates the Arab world — even if one does have to grant that it helped preserve Islam.

Can this tendency to lay claim to the old provinces of historic Syria be qualified as a form of imperialism, however? Not quite. In every Arab subconscious, individually or collectively, there exists a drive towards unity which is constantly struggling against individual sectarianism and tribalism. There is the dim memory of the glorious empire of the Arab-Islamic Caliphate. And yet, it cannot be stressed enough, the Arab Ba'ath Party played its part in disrupting the union between Egypt and Syria. The narrow egocentrism of the party and the individualism of its leaders prevailed over the Ba'athist unionist ideology. Indeed it is possible that the Syrian regime's sub-conscious guilt at having contributed to the disintegration of the United Arab Republic was partly behind the rapprochement with Jordan and the military intervention in Lebanon, to the detriment of the historic alliance with Egypt. It is also probable that, with Sleiman Frangie in power, the Syrian leaders thought that it would be easy to turn Lebanon into a satellite state even if it did escape the noose of a Syrian confederacy. For President Assad, as I see it, Lebanon was a diplomatic wager of the first importance, a trump card, an asset to be traded off in negotiations with the U.S., the U.S.S.R. and Europe, with a view to securing a satisfactory settlement of the problem of Syria's frontiers and of the territories occupied by Israel. Lebanon was supposed to give Syria the diplomatic prestige it needed on the international scene.

Furthermore, Syria's Army was over-armed with tanks, yet could not permit itself the luxury of attacking Israel. The regime gave in to the tempta-tion of holding its military parades in Lebanon. These and other material factors certainly played as great a role in the events as the individual and collective subconscious, even if in the last analysis, human action always stems from the psyche. Only a brilliant success could extract the regime from the impasse it had driven into. I dread the day when the Arabs will be finished (theoretically) with Israel. What bloody games, what internecine wars will they indulge in then? Unless, of course, the long-awaited new Bismarck finally emerges. As Toynbee says, Gamal Abd el-Nasser played this role for us, but unfortunately (thanks to the Arab leaders themselves and the Syrians in particular) he failed to realize the unity of the Arab nation, perhaps because this nation does not yet exist and is still, as in the days of the Caliphate, only a *commonwealth* of peoples. For these various peoples to become a true nation, they will have to gain a better understanding of their rich and glorious past, and transcend or sublimate their individualism.

The Syrian leaders' interest in Lebanon became especially manifest during the election of the new President of the Republic, through the pressures they exercised, the funds they used to get Elias Sarkis elected, but especially in their uncomprehending and venomous attitude towards the other candidate, Raymond Edde. We were beginning to learn where we stood. Having failed to impose their 'political solution', which had, in the end, been accepted by the Gemayel-Frangie-Shamun clan and — despite certain highly justified reserva-tions — even by ourselves, the Syrians could have explored other avenues before sending their army against Islam, the Lebanese left and the indepen-dent Christian leaders. But President Assad saw things differently. He said quite openly (even to us) that, to maintain a presence in Lebanon, one first had to win over the Maronites — those whom he himself designated as the isolationists — rather than the patriots. As he put it, this was an 'historic opportunity'. And he sacrificed us on that altar. We were the paschal lamb offered up to secure this alliance; henceforth, we must remember to celebrate Easter . . . . Every Muslim Arab has an inferiority complex *vis-a-vis* the Maronites, whether it be as a result of a lack of understanding or out of some superficial wish to appear liberal and magnanimous. Only the Druses knew how to handle the destructive, hypocritical and rebellious isolationists; the strong arm when it was required, and benevolence when it was reasonable.

Although Syria helped us politically at the beginning of the war, they did so only very tentatively, without ever breaking off with the other side. In their effort to present themselves as the epitome of conciliation, they displayed towards our enemies a special clemency, a bizarre partiality. As for military assistance, to be blunt, we received practically nothing. We bought our weapons ourselves, the people bought them. They merely passed through Syria. Nor did we ever ask for financial help; we were conscious of the Syrian people's financial difficulties. So we owe them really very little, especially as the Syrian leaders were actually holding up deliveries of the weapons and munitions stockpiled on our behalf in Syria. It was a way of exercising indirect pressure upon us, of manipulating us; they seemed to want to make the war drag on unnecessarily. We had to insist very vehemently to get the blockade lifted. The Syrians seemed determined — especially towards the end — to maintain an equilibrium between the contending forces in Lebanon, no doubt with the idea that they would thereby make their task easier when they finally lanced their abcess of Lebanon. Malicious rumours suggest that President Frangie received a gift of weapons from Syria before events got underway. It is also said that, at about the same time, truckloads of guns and ammunition for the isolationists were crossing Syria from Jordan, where the Falangists were being trained in the use of semi-heavy weapons. Later the Saika, too, gave a similar helping hand to their friends, the Kataeb. As for the cannons, those famous 160mm mortars, it seems probable that the Lebanese right got them from Israel. One day, we will find out what basis there is for all these rumours . . . . In the meanwhile, the Arabs looked on from afar, as if they were spectators at a cockfight.

There is no doubt in my mind that racist religious fascism must first be crushed militarily and then cared for psychologically. I remember my last interview with President Assad, when I refused to call an immediate cessation of hostilities. Obviously he was displeased, but it did not warrant so violent a reaction on his part, namely open warfare against the National Movement and the humiliation of the left and of Islam in Lebanon. Perhaps we upset his plans. I was only asking for a few days grace, a week or two at the very most, before declaring an armistice. Just time enough to free Dhour Choueir and Baskinta, where our partisans were surrounded. We were convinced that only our military victory could put an end to the isolationists' war. We had to act quickly: Israel and its press were bemoaning the fate of the Lebanese right, 'abandoned' by Europe and the United States. At Reyfoun, which had been declared an open city, we would have received their surrender and signed the armistice. Later, we could have, and indeed would have had a duty to be liberal and magnanimous towards them.

During this last conversation, President Assad expressed himself very frankly: 'Listen,' he said, 'for me, this is an historic opportunity to re-orient

the Maronites towards Syria, to win their trust, to make them realize that
their source of protection is no longer France or the West. They have to be
helped to stop going to beg for help abroad. I cannot allow you to defeat the
Christian camp in Lebanon; they would be permanently embittered.'

'But we are not talking about the Christian camp,' I replied. 'Do not
forget, Mr. President, that the Greek Orthodox, the Armenians, three-quarters
of the Greek Catholics and a third of the Maronites themselves are hostile
to the attitudes of the ultras of Maronite isolationism. That makes more than
two-thirds of the Christians in Lebanon. They have to be saved from the
fascist yoke; all these isolationists represent less than 25% of the Christians.'

'Nonetheless, I cannot allow you to beat the isolationists, I would not
want them to feel they had been defeated', he replied sharply. And he kept
coming back to the same slogan: these people would no longer turn to
Europe or the United States but to the Arabs and Syria instead. A bad cal-
culation and a total lack of understanding of Lebanon's problem! An illusion and an alibi! He felt it was his national duty as an Arab to disengage
the Maronites from the magic protective circle of France and Europe.

Was he sincere? At the time, he seemed to be, but who would say so
lately? Politics is not charity. At first, admittedly, his *tour de force*
succeeded, but eventually Maronite suspicions prevailed. Arab-Muslim
occupation always frightens the Maronites, especially if the occupying forces
are the Syrians, whom they have always considered as their worst enemies.
The Maronites' nightmare is that, once the Syrians have entered the region,
they will not leave it again. There was an outcry when the Syrians marched
into Beirut and the Metn. In fact, it is neither the Muslims nor the patriotic
Christians who express the greatest reservations about the Syrian aggression;
the isolationists are the ones who are the most appalled by what has
happened. Especially now that the Syrians are here, they can forget their
dreams of partition and a little Maronite state. Stubborn and obtuse, the
isolationists are often slow to understand the consequences of their actions.
Calm co-operation and good intentions may predominate on the surface, but
already popular feeling is beginning to rise; doubt and fear are spreading. It
is thanks to this doubt and fear that the Israelis have been able to penetrate
the isolationists and manipulate them (look at what is happening in South
Lebanon). When one contemplates the fanaticism and psychological
complexes of nearly all the Lebanese religious communities, one can
easily despair and feel that perhaps our dream of unification is more utopian
than practical. And then, hope revives. Did President Assad, with his
soldier's sense of realism, experience similar feelings?

The whole enterprise is a wager. Can one really expect this bizarre alliance
between the Syrians and the Maronites, who are Israel's allies, to last?
Damascus may have a difficult hand to play, but President Assad obviously
has more than one card up his sleeve. Syrian public opinion, the army and
some members of the Ba'ath are very concerned. Nonetheless, peoples who
have been deprived of freedom rarely rediscover its uses either speedily or
easily, especially when they are surrounded by thousands of police spies,

and bombarded with official propaganda. Given this mini-totalitarianism, President Assad relies much more on secrecy, deviousness, apathy and on his own skill at wearing an obstacle down bit by bit, than on securing the understanding or support of public opinion.

Why did Syria abandon us? Once again, I detect a psychological rather than a political factor at work: we were deemed too independent. We have never been in the pay of the U.S., the U.S.S.R. or anybody else. Our method of action was too dynamic and out of proportion to the importance of the Progressive Socialist Party and its allies. We had our own clearly defined ideas about the Arabs, Arabism and the various problems of the Arab world. We put our case politely, tactfully even, but honestly. As our Syrian ex-allies once put it, we seemed likely to lead them where they did not wish to go, namely towards political democracy and away from Geneva — or rather towards a real Geneva. We had a realistic view of the Palestinian problem and its solution: no compromise with the Hebrew State will be valid unless it includes the return of the 1,200,000 refugees to their houses, their lands and their work in Israel (in short, the implementation of the 1946-47 U.N. resolutions). This is also the only way to resolve the Lebanese problem. (Nearly 350,000 Palestinians are in Lebanon, and there will be 800,000 in 10 or 12 years.)

We were too turbulent. The Arab world refused to be shaken out of its lethargy. The Nasserist adventure still frightened the existing rulers. The oil potentates resented us for demanding that they participate in the drive for Arab salvation. Syria dreaded new problems on its flanks.

Instead of support, we were served up an aphorism: 'Syrian security and Lebanese security are interdependent.' Just about everybody was afraid of change in Lebanon, afraid of its consequences and the problems it might entail. Also, Lebanon would have ceased to be that eternal pleasure garden to which all rich and influential Arabs could come to slake their thirst for pleasure, fulminating all the while about its vices and demanding change; Arab phariseeism and 'progressive' hypocrisy has rarely had such fine representatives. Some people, in Arabia for example, were concerned that we might pave the way for communism, and the propaganda broadcasts by the Syrians (who are, let us not forget, allied to the communists in government) did everything to implant this fear amongst those who were influential in Saudi Arabia, the Gulf, Egypt and elsewhere. The Americans, Israel and the B.B.C. did likewise. Our effective moral independence and our growing influence over Arab public opinion caused a panic. And finally, it was clear that we would have to be disciplined before the Palestinians could be brought to heel. It is always dangerous to go against the tacit and ambiguous intentions of the seraglios. We only just got out of it alive. But we did our duty, we created a wave which will one day determine the Arab future.

To come back to the isolationists and the strategic evolution of the Lebanese crisis, the Maronite minority has now distanced itself from Syria and has turned increasingly towards Israel. Yet in the long term, the Maronites' real interest, and the interest of every other minority in the region, is to remain the faithful and moral allies of the adherents of Arabism. Many of them live in fear: 'At the moment, as long as Hafez el-Assad and his regime are in power, everything is fine; the Syrian troops have moved in and are going to hammer the Palestinians and the Lebanese left. But should the regime in Syria suddenly fall, or change its policy, we would be lost.'

These are still only vague apprehensions, and yet I have noticed that Bechir Gemayel, Shamun, the clergy and the ordinary people are none too happy with what is happening. They are constantly asking themselves questions, reinforcing their alliance with the Jewish State and sending emissaries everywhere, to the United States, to Israel, to Europe and also to Damascus. The Israeli artillery's intervention in the south, to protect the little semi-independent enclave of Kleya and Marjeyoun, raised their hopes and their spirits. They play Israel off against Syria, without breaking with the Syrians for all that. The manoeuvre is very skilful: the Syrians are effectively being denied access to South Lebanon, and are being openly challenged, along with all the Arabs. The isolationists, with Israeli help, have given their Syrian Arab friends and protectors a slap in the face. As a gesture of gratitude and friendship, it is worth noting.

Strangely enough, Syria is probably the only country never to have had an embassy in Lebanon. This anomaly stems from considerations prevailing before 1943, in other words before the National Pact agreement which preceded the emergence of Lebanon.

Following the creation of the State of Lebanon in 1919, the Lebanese people, as part of their struggle for independence, demanded union with Syria. In the four *cazas* which had been returned to Lebanon, including Beirut, the population, which had been cut off from the Mountain, an autonomous *sandjak*[2] since 1864, expressed their wish to be reintegrated into Syria. Syrian nationalism was running high, whipped on by the Arabism of the Sherifs and Lawrence. It provided the slogan and the pretext to oppose the French Mandate. In any case, the old Arab emirate of Lebanon, which had been resuscitated in the context of French and Maronite domination, had little in common with its former self. Historically, it had been the Djebel Druses, now it was the Mountain or the Maronite principality. Its lord had been the Caliph of Istanbul, who always kept more or less in the background; now it was ruled by France, the traditional protector of the Maronites. The Islamic Druse orientation, which operated in the context of the historical Syria, had been replaced by a sort of small French *departement* on the Syrian coast. Around this time, Dr. Edmond Rabbat wrote his book on the United Arab States. Both Christian and Muslim leaders were involved in the movement. The real project of the patriots, who were organized into secret societies from the middle of the 19th Century up to the beginning of the 20th Century, was to establish a semi-autonomous Lebanon linked to Syria within the context of an independent Greater Syria.

Antoun Saade's Syrian Popular Party was eventually grafted onto this historical movement. The current of protest lasted right up to the period just before independence and was very much in keeping with the spirit of a period which saw the emergence of German and Italian nationalism in Europe. One should bear in mind that, historically, the autonomy secured for these coastal provinces by the Druses and Sunni Emirs had always been achieved within the framework of historical Syria. Lebanon, even before it was so named, was in a way Syria's Prussia. Just before independence, a compromise finally emerged. The Syrian Unionists and the moderate Maronites made substantial mutual concessions: the result was the famous National Pact. A majority of Maronites gave up the idea of prolonging the French Mandate, whilst a majority of Unionists renounced their ambitions for immediate and complete integration with Damascus, even if they kept the dream of an Arab union alive in the depths of their heart.

But the concessions granted to the Maronites were more psychological than real and practical. An adequate understanding of common interests soon led to the setting up of an effective customs union, and indeed to a form of economic unity between Syria and Lebanon. Free movement of goods, persons and capital between the two was maintained until a personal conflict divided the Lebanese Prime Minister, Mr. Riad Solh and the then Syrian President of the Council, Khaled el-Azm. Furthermore, the National Pact had tacitly laid down that Beirut and Damascus would not exchange diplomatic representatives, so as not to offend the sensibilities of the Lebanese Unionists. It became customary to hold conferences at which joint foreign policy was decided. The divergences between Syria and Lebanon only emerged later, when the common interests policy was abolished and when a new economic regime was installed in Damascus: joint decision-making then became much less frequent. Later still, Gamal Abd el-Nasser's realization of the Syrian-Egyptian Union had a profound effect on people in Lebanon — just like everywhere else — and helped to revive the Arab unionist current (on a theoretical and verbal level, at least). But ultra-Maronitism, fuelled, as always, by the fear of Islam and Arabism, was also profoundly marked by Nasser's initiative. Relations between the various communities in Lebanon suffered in consequence, despite the (rather curious) fact that nearly all the Arab unionist parties, including the Ba'ath, had originally been founded by Christians.

To come back to the present, the support Damascus has provided for the Maronites carries many indirect dangers for the Syrian regime. Let us not forget that Syria too is governed by a minority, the Alawites. In the past, this community were denied access to the centre of power, but their considerable intelligence has recently won them a preponderant influence within the State, the Party and the administration. Recent major projects in Alawrite country have included irrigation, road-building, land improvement and the development of the ports of Lattaquie, Djebleh and Tartous. Alawites have flowed into Homs in large numbers and now form the majority in the town, which would probably become the capital of an eventual Alawite State if one ever came into existence, and if their other political wing ever agreed to such a venture. They have also steadily infiltrated the coastal areas, especially around Lattaquie. The population of these

Alawite or Alawitized areas is undoubtedly far more confident in its future than ever before.

But I do not think that, originally, Damascus really intended to support the isolationists' efforts in Lebanon. The Syrians simply wanted to appear as the arbiters of the conflict and then as the protectors of the Maronite nation. As it turned out, however, the Maronites manipulated them into serving the ends of the little confessional homeland they wanted to create. Once again, the feelings of the Syrian leaders overruled their judgement: there was far more resentment and rancour than logic or rationality in the Syrian decisions. Circumstances and Syrian pigheadedness helped the Maronites against the parties of the Lebanese left, against the nationalist movement, against all those who opposed the Syrian plan to turn Lebanon into a satellite state without having to fight for it. This vindictiveness was so pronounced that, only a few months ago, Minister Khaddam could be heard to say: 'The true patriots in Lebanon are the "people of the Kfour".' Such a statement by a Syrian nationalist carries heavy implications. It makes one realize just how dishonest, clumsy and obtuse ex-President Frangie must have been to invite the Syrian intervention. Now that the Syrians are in Lebanon, we shall see if they intend to carry on with this course, if they will really back the partition of Lebanon or the creation of a confessional Maronite State within a disunited Lebanon, or whether they will be tempted to realize their territorial ambitions concerning the north and east of Lebanon, the Akkar and the Bekaa. The Israelis would welcome such a move, because it would enable them to lay hands on part of Southern Lebanon.

All these various ambitions are interconnected. In the end, however, everything depends on the position of the West, and especially on the United States. The dismemberment of Lebanon will be no easy matter. Are we to be a new Czechoslovakia, a new Poland? I do not think that the Cypriot precedent is likely to apply in Lebanon. The context is different and the Arabs will not tolerate such an attitude on the part of the U.S. For the moment, the Americans seem not to be in favour of partition, but one can never be sure. Israel, too, has no interest in pushing the game to its limits; a divided Lebanon would mean Syrian troops stationed along much of the present Lebanese–Israeli borders, and that would present a real threat to Israel – Nakouara and Chebaa are far too close to the Israeli towns. So I think that everything will be up for renegotiation; we will not suffer Poland's fate.

A better understanding of the Lebanese problem might also help the U.S.S.R. to adopt a firmer position. What confuses the U.S.S.R., and everybody else, is that Arab opinion, which was originally strongly opposed to the Syrian military intervention, ended up by tolerating if not applauding it. There are so many paradoxes in this Arab world. The U.S.S.R. feels that the Lebanese Communist Party is still too weak to assume power. Nonetheless, the Soviet Union does not fully appreciate the importance of the development of political democracy in Lebanon and its potential consequences in the Arab world. If the Soviets had intervened positively in the Lebanese conflict, they could have completely re-established their political position in the Arab world. Water under the bridge . . . .

I do not know if the Soviet Union looks at Lebanese political thinking in the same way that we do. Lebanon is probably the only Arab country — outside North Africa, at least — where real political thought exists, even if it is not precisely Marxist. Does the U.S.S.R. believe, as we do, that the economic, social and political evolution precipitated by the events of 1975-76 will transform the Lebanese problem and push things towards progressivism, despite the present reactionary upsurge which is, paradoxically enough, being encouraged by the progressives of Syria and elsewhere? At the moment, Maronite propaganda in favour of partition is abating. But the demands for autonomy, political decentralization and a cantonal system are making headway, and could serve as the prelude to partition. The little *de facto* buffer state in the south actively encourages this tendency. Shamun, along with Israel, is pushing for such an outcome more intensely than any of the other Kfour leaders. Pierre Gemayel and his Falangists seem to be weary of the problems involved in administering Kesruan and Jbeil, but his son, Bechir, apparently feels differently, despite a certain ambiguity. However, the leaders of ultra-Maronitism tend to egg each other on and are constantly forced to raise the stakes. In practice, as I said, everything depends on the U.S. and on whether the Americans are still genuinely committed to an undivided Lebanon. A little Maronite State can only emerge with the agreement of the great powers, perhaps even of all the powers involved.

Unfortunately, President Sarkis, deprived of his army and forced to rely on the mainly Syrian Arab army, can do very little given the present conditions; the administration, the police, the army, the courts, everything has collapsed into chaos. Apparently, he is not too worried, but that seems difficult to believe. His first task is obviously to draw the nation together again, so that we may become truly efficient and independent. Perhaps we could be as calm as he is if we felt we could trust certain Syrian declarations. But we do not intend to learn again the hard way that nothing is free in politics. If the Syrians are genuinely devoid of ulterior motives, why have they broken with the National Movement and the Lebanese left?

And what about the Phoenician spirit, now dormant but once so preponderant amongst the Maronites? What has happened to all the carpet salesmen, the shopkeepers, big and small, the import-export agents buying and selling on the world market from their offices in Beirut? Is it not likely that the taste for lucre, for financial wheeling and dealing will eventually prevail over the crusader spirit (not that the old-time Crusaders in Lebanon were motivated exclusively by their religious ideals — they often came with the very down-to-earth intention of making their fortune)? Will there be a reaction along these lines? Under the circumstances, it would be quite healthy, but somehow I think it unlikely. The isolationists have been given too much encouragement by Damascus. Syria would now have to take drastic steps to convince them to change course.

What will happen? Will Hafez el-Assad persist with his project of reconstructing Greater Syria? I cannot tell, but whatever happens, Lebanon will certainly remain an abnormal entity, unless the Lebanese refamiliarize themselves with the Lebanese idea (as they once succeeded in doing) and manage to transform it into a single, undivided and progressive nation.

A natural Syria, realized with the consent of the population and with due respect for democracy, might *in extremis* be acceptable to Lebanon; but that would imply that the problem of democracy and political stability in Damascus had already been solved. Certainly, at present, no Lebanese wishes to become a Syrian. Why should we consent to walk into that great prison pullulating with agents of the secret police? (According to a recent report, there are 49,000 of them, an utterly ridiculous number.) Furthermore, Lebanon cannot be integrated into Syria just like that. It would have to have a special status, because over time the Lebanese have developed a character and spirit which are very much their own and quite different from those of the Syrians. On the other hand, many Syrians would dearly like to be Lebanese. This has always been the case throughout history: a special status was granted Lebanon within the framework of Ottoman Syria. As I have already noted, Lebanon seems to have served as Syria's Prussia, perhaps because it was the most dynamic element within the Syrian context. Fakhr el-Din II, Prince of Lebanon (the Druse *jebel*), united all Syria under his authority. This dynamism was even more manifest prior to 1585, the year the *Wali* of Egypt, Ibrahim Pasha, massacred 60,000 Druses. After that, Druse influence in Lebanon declined, even though they were the true initiators of the country's move towards independence. The *Wali* of Egypt was abetted in his butchery by Ahmed el-Hafez, the *Wali* of Damascus.

The Lebanese have lived separate from Syria for nearly 60 years now, or for over a hundred years if one goes back to 1864. Over that period, they have learnt to be much more concerned with their own country's affairs than with fusion with a neighbouring State. In time, a subconscious collective bond developed, which opened up the possibility of a united Lebanese people who could transcend political confessionalism. The isolationists' great failing is their tendency to close themselves off and refuse to see what is happening around them. Lebanese democracy could evolve within a framework established by the parties and public opinion. Lebanese unity would be reinforced as a result, and so would the Lebanese structure itself, the independence of Lebanon and the bonds which tie its citizens to their small country.

But will the Syrians allow us to implement these policies, will they help us carry them through? They have already attacked the freedom of the press; that is a bad omen, but I wager that they will eventually have to backtrack. If we survive, if these reforms are introduced, if we can have democracy, convince the traditionalists, change their mistaken ideas, strip them of their petty and paradoxical disguise, we will have won a considerable political victory, even if it takes us five or ten years. But if Syria maintains its present position, it will be very difficult for us to implement the slightest significant reform, let alone anything resembling the first step towards a truly radical reform. Following the fall of Nabau, the invasion of the Upper Metn and Sannine, and the deployment of Syrian troops throughout the country (except in Southern Lebanon) one is forced to ask oneself whether any of this is still possible. The counter-revolution will gradually fall apart or will be brushed aside. The months to come will, I feel, be decisive, and we shall see whether the country is ready for rejuvenation or whether the old ideas prevail. The silent struggle of honest people against mercantilism and political opportunism will go on, even if the Syrian presence and the need to concentrate on preserving our independence pushes it into the background. The political and military struggle which has been waged over the last two years has broadened political consciousness generally. I repeat: it was the military offensive launched against us by the Syrians in November 1976 which encouraged the ultra-Maronites to pursue their ambitions and allowed Israel to intervene, both directly and indirectly, in Lebanon. But many nations have gone through what we are going through. If the ideal of unity prevails, if the people who have struggled for unity manage to have the last word in the country's political affairs, then we will win what others have secured for themselves. Sooner or later, the revolution will triumph. And yet, the adventure will have been worthwhile.

Notes

1. Black September.
2. An Ottoman administrative area.

6. Dialogue: Philip Lapousterle and Kamal Joumblatt

Philippe Lapousterle: *Lebanon has just emerged from two years of war. What do you see as the consequences of that war?*

Kamal Joumblatt: I wonder if the country has really emerged from these two years of violent crisis. People have still not returned to their homes (I am thinking of the refugees on both sides); there is a kind of moral or psychic wall that still separates the two communities and prevents any resettlement.

What has changed? I feel that at this stage one can only give a very tentative answer. It would seem that the main purpose of the Syrian intervention was to maintain a certain *status quo* in terms of Lebanon's political and economic institutions. But will that be enough for Damascus, or do the Syrians intend to exercise a long lasting political mandate over Lebanon? In that case, there will be no major change: we will increasingly be drawn into the Arab 'world of silence' and our liberties will steadily be curtailed, because the policy throughout the region, in Syria as elsewhere, is to deny public opinion a voice. The problem of democracy is crucial. To what extent will it be maintained, what obstacles will be put in its path, what 'legal' limitations will be voted through or imposed? The present battle for freedom of the press will indicate the direction in which things are moving, because even those amongst the isolationists who are most content with the turn of events are liable, I think, to be hit by similar measures: liberty in a country is indivisible. Will these restrictions on their freedom encourage the Lebanese to rebel? One can only speculate.

At the moment, people are tired after two years of battles, and Damascus is taking advantage of the fact in order to establish its influence over Lebanon more firmly. Perhaps the Syrians are frightened that freedom of the press will spread into Syria, where it is one of the main demands of public opinion. After freedom of the press, the next question will be the freedom of the parties. Will the major foreign powers such as Europe and the U.S. allow President Assad a free hand? None of these problems will be easily resolved, and it is difficult to predict their outcome. In any case, if proof is needed, the imposition of censorship in Lebanon demonstrates the crisis of the Damascus regime. On the other side of the wall of silence, the authorities are frightened that Lebanon's examples might attract some disciples.

The silence imposed is also meant to pave the way to Geneva, by forcing the Palestinians to keep quiet as well. What attitude will President Sarkis adopt? Will he accept this series of little *coup d'etats* whose aim is to destroy Lebanese democracy? I know him to be a democrat. Will he suffer the same fate as Benes in Czechoslovakia? I cannot say for sure, but of one thing I am quite certain, the people of my country are deeply attached to their freedom and will do what they can to hang on to it. Will the Arab League, in theory the final authority over the Arab intervention forces, manage to curb Syria's federal ambitions? It is too early to tell what our future political status will be, but it will undoubtedly change, probably along the lines set out in former President Frangie's so-called Constitutional Message. But what will be the role of the parties in this new context? It all still remains open to debate.

So why the 50,000 dead and 100,000 wounded in Lebanon?

They will have fallen in order to allow the Syrians to say 'Stop the battle'. They will have fallen to justify Damascus's efforts to impose its influence on Lebanon by organizing the Saika, by developing a secret network of agents throughout the country and, later perhaps, by insisting upon a mutual security pact. We do not know the Syrian regime's precise present intentions, but we have learnt over time that it rarely changes its line. It remains to be seen if Saudi Arabia wants to do something: she certainly can, and so can Egypt. (I will not hide the fact that we have appealed to President Sadat to initiate a frank exchange of views with President Assad on the subject of Lebanon.) I think that President Sarkis has placed far too much faith in the Syrians' good intentions.

There are few examples in history of a revolutionary movement controlling a substantial area of the national territory. You held power for two years in Saida, for more than a year in Tripoli and for nearly six months in parts of Beirut. The problem is that you do not seem to have done very much in the territories you controlled.

That is true. It was extremely difficult to do anything given the anarchy of the organizations and parties. At first, we were always waiting for this insane war to stop, for peace to be established so that we could reach some sort of compromise. We were short of weapons and the Palestinians were none too keen on our military independence. The Syrians were close on our heels and we had to secure the agreement of 13 different parties before we could take any decision of the slightest importance. Furthermore, we deliberately resisted creating a local administration so as to avoid encouraging the other camp to do likewise and thereby invoking a climate of partition. The Vietnamese example does not apply; the context is entirely different. As for economic and social reforms (agrarian reform, redistribution of land and housing) I myself was in favour of going ahead with them, but other left parties were not. All the potentates and magnates of the Arab world would have been furious and we would have been gobbled up even sooner, especially by the supposedly progressive Arab regimes. I felt that we should take the risk nonetheless, but too many others disagreed. So it is quite true that we did very little. Towards the end, we had just begun to organize a rudimentary system of administration, policing and justice. We were pragmatic throughout: daily worries, weekly efforts and monthly plans seemed enough. I must admit that, in this area, I was a little lazy. We were all psychologically and physically exhausted. And our primary concern was always, as I have said, to preserve the country's unity.

Yet one has to look at things as they are. For the next thirty years, people may be telling you: 'We saw what you did when you were in power . . .'

Perhaps. But I repeat, the unity and integrity of the country were paramount; they were higher on our list of priorities than the need to govern or to implement reforms which would in any case probably turn out to be only temporary. Do not forget that what we were fighting for was the maintenance of this unity, the implementation of democratic reforms and the security of the Palestinian movement. If these three objectives have been attained, I feel that, for the moment, we have succeeded, despite the strength of the Israeli-American plot, Syria's antagonism, and what I would call our betrayal by progressive forces internationally. Neither China nor the Soviet Union backed us; we are not Vietnam. Remember also, that apart from the 13 parties and groups which made up the National Movement, we had to take into account a whole range of other leftists and especially something like a dozen different Palestinian organizations, most of whom lived on the margins of the law. Believe me, cadres were one thing the Progressive Socialist Party was never short of, and we probably should have reinforced our position within the organizational structure of the National Movement. But we were reluctant to press our claims too hard.

La Fontaine says, 'As long as all is deliberation, counsellors at Court abound; as soon as things are to be done, no one can be found.' The National Movement was notable for daily meetings which lasted five, six or even seven hours, with very little practical result. How does one explain this hiatus between the number of meetings and the low level of achievement?

In the Middle East, in any meeting, speechifying usually prevails at first. One has to give the Devil his due. Eventually, people realize that less talk is essential; I think we were getting to that stage. One is either time's victim or its master. We were about to appoint an executive council, but the tragedy of the invasion forced us to put off its election. Those on the other side were still at the talking-shop stage. I repeat, we were 13 in this league of parties, and we always had to take into account so many tendencies, vagaries, the different Arab backers of the different groups. We had problems, especially in Beirut, with the re-emergence of the traditional personalities and with the disparate tendencies within the Arab Lebanese Army. Many people find it difficult to move towards socialism without chafing at the bit. We also had to watch out for counter-revolutionary activities based on agents of the isolationist front within our ranks, on the Beirut Islamic League, on Mr. Saeb Salam's front and on the divergences within the little Arab Lebanese Army. The American, Israeli, Syrian and Jordanian intelligence services were endlessly busy. They all sought to prevent us from exercising effective authority and to make life as difficult as possible for us. But it has to be admitted that some of the main problems we faced were due to the rivalries, secret competition and, occasionally, outright antagonism between the parties that made up our alliance.

You are the leader of the Progressive Socialist Party which, after a few months of struggle, joined with other groups to form the National Movement. Why did you avoid words such as 'revolutionary' or even 'progressive' when it came to naming the new organization?

We chose the name ourselves. We tried to avoid words which might have pointlessly offended sections of public opinion in Lebanon and the Arab world. Also, the term 'revolutionary' has been bandied about far too much in the area. One can be a revolutionary without sounding a fanfare about it. And evolution is always better than revolution, especially where it is a matter of safeguarding human rights and civil liberties. The political programme of the new democratic system we are proposing links and unites us. An economic, social and cultural programme will follow. This formula is a substantial step forward towards a real front. We had to unite Lebanon's political activists, and, as far as possible, to unite their military operations as well, if we were to gain some independence *vis-a-vis* the Palestinian revolution, to whom we could well have been an embarrassment from time to time. We could easily have fallen into organizational anarchy. One has to be independent in order to implement reforms and lay the foundations of a real revolution. Our political aims may not always match those of the Palestinians. For them, anarchy may at times be more profitable than organization. Furthermore, they have a mistaken conception of all these supposedly progressive regimes of the Arab world. Their primary concern is to safeguard the Palestinian Revolution. They have lost Tel el-Zatar and are now being pursued and harassed by the Syrians; their main objective now must be to gain time, to resist passively while they reorganize. We all need to work like moles during this interlude. Assad's regime is tenacious and inflexibly vindictive, but its sense of realism should not be underestimated. Better times may be on the horizon. The recent events in Egypt are a good sign, and at the moment, President Assad seems somewhat more amenable.

If I had to define your position during this crisis, I would call you the eminence grise *of the Palestinian Resistance rather than the leader of the Lebanese National Movement.*

In a way, you would be right. The Progressive Socialist Party and I jointly formulated the common political programme of the Lebanese left and the P.L.O. in an effort to 'catch' the Lebanese and shake them up a bit, so that this bloody war might at least have some positive results. We had to face up to the problem of the antagonisms between Lebanese and Lebanese, otherwise it would have been framed in terms of a conflict between Lebanese and Palestinian. We struggled to impose our point of view on certain parties because it was urgent to define a political goal for the Lebanese masses and because the fundamental problem was really the social conflict between privileged and non-privileged Lebanese: the Whites and the Blacks of Zimbabwe so to speak. The Lebanese have sacrificed so much, it would have been terrible for it all to count for nothing. We realized right from the start that the Syrian presence would be an obstacle to the implementation of our programme. On top of which, there were so many twitching egos, so many petty ambitions unleashed — politics is a fairly dirty business. Those who were sympathetic towards us at the time nevertheless remained reserved and distant. They wanted no distractions from their furious propaganda war against Sadat's Egypt and the Sinai Agreements. In Syria, as in the rest of the Arab world, almost none of the leaders was really interested in what we were trying to do for our democracy. The Syrians were concerned only with the Golan, and the over-rich Arabs cared only for the construction of their cities and their palaces, the arrangement and permanence of their well-being: their problem was simply how best to waste their oil money. Islam in Lebanon, led by the mullahs and traditional chieftains, was, as always, resistant to secularization; on the other side, the isolationist Christians would not give up their confessional and political privileges but offered the Muslims a secular state which most of the latter wanted nothing to do with. The whole thing was a maze!

Even the 'progressive' President of Syria was publicly declaiming against political secularization. Certain left parties and small groups of every variety panicked and started rushing about calling for class struggle, in a country which has barely 70,000 industrial workers, a great many of whom were fighting on the other side. In Lebanon, where American-style embourgeoisement has spread throughout the social classes, ideologies often completely cloud the critical faculties of many intellectuals and party men. The opium of ideology is frequently more noxious than the opium of religion. And the Arab rulers pronounced anathema upon us because the communists had acquired a prominent position in the central councils of this mish-mash of parties and groups. As for the Lebanese people, most of them were sick of a struggle which had led to so many immoral, criminal and barbarous acts. In this sewer of ferocity and bloody banditry (the true face of this Western civilization, in the third phase of its economic and social evolution), one had both to defend oneself and to fight for an ideal. Yet one could not help feeling confused, ashamed even, at all the filthy things that were being done on the margins of our struggle and in its name. Naturally and spontaneously, one felt moved by a deep pity for all those who were dying every day, cut down like human grass by the intense bombardments. And all to defend a democracy which nobody in the Arab world seemed to care much about, even amongst the countries which were helping us.

Suddenly, the brutal aspect of revolution had interposed itself between the Lebanese intelligentsia and the revolutionary dream they had once cherished. In Lebanon, all the young people, all the leftists, had dreamed of revolution, all the parties and groups competed as to who could use the words 'revolutionary' and 'revolution' the most. Revolution was *de rigueur*, even in dress and appearance: tousled hair, no tie, a carefully maintained layer of grime. Gilded youth and juvenile delinquents threw themselves wholeheartedly into the game. Poor old Marx and Lenin must have been reeling in their graves. And yet, despite all this, the basis remained serious, sincere and truly moving.

On 22 January 1976, during the minimally respected ceasefire, everything seemed to be about to return to normal. But it was all thrown into turmoil again, firstly by the creation of the Army of Arab Lebanon, and secondly by the attack on the villages of Mount Lebanon. Your own position is well-known: you sought to force those whom you call the isolationists to surrender. What is more difficult to understand is the stance taken by Yasser Arafat, who must have known that he would thereby lose the support of the Syrians.

Let us go back a bit, if you will. The first armistice, in 1975, was brought down by the Saika following the formation of the Karame Government, when the Syrians sought to exclude the arbitration of the Saudi, Kuwaiti and Egyptian ambassadors, in order to remain in sole possession of the terrain and impose their own solution.

As for the little Army of Arab Lebanon, it formed itself quite spontaneously. The Palestinians and their allies had pursued the unfortunate idea of seizing the Hasbaya barracks and seraglio. Lieutenant Khatib, a patriotic young officer with a good sense of politics, took advantage of the occasion; feeling that the General Staff was penalizing him for his ideas, he rebelled, insisting most forcefully that the Army should remain neutral in the conflict. Spontaneously, or as a result of hidden pressure — it has been said that certain Palestinians and irresponsible groups triggered off the movement — the barracks quickly fell to his cause, one after another. The young lieutenant had been in contact with us previously, through his father and his cousin, Zaher el-Khatib. For several months we strove to dissuade him from this sterile adventure and later we tried to prevent the constant rebellions of soldiers and non-commissioned officers. But a kind of military and social democracy was emerging and the movement steadily grew. People were playing with fire without realizing it. Until then, we had managed to preserve the unity of the Lebanese Army, which could have played an important role in keeping the peace once things had settled down and a political solution had emerged. It might have saved us from the bad times we are going through now . . . .

Yet Ahmed el-Khatib is one of your people, is he not?

No. He is simply the cousin of the socialist deputy Zaher el-Khatib; both he and the lieutenant's father have repeatedly contacted me to ask, 'Should Ahmed leave the Army?' My answer was always, 'No, he should stay; it is always better to fight from the inside than from the outside; the Army must not be allowed to fall apart.' This has always been my approach. I saw little future for a small rebel army led by under-qualified officers. The episode had very little in common with what happened on the *Potemkin* [during the Russian Revolution].

At first, the Syrian officers encouraged us to keep the Army in one piece. It was only later, when it was about to fall apart, that they advised us to draw on the officers, non-commissioned officers and soldiers as the framework for our militias, just as the other side had already done. Once the Army had broken up due to the blind, confessionalist and disorganized behaviour of General Iskandar Ghanem, its commanding officer, and once Khatib and his comrades had left, it was only normal that we should support the symbol of Arab Lebanon that his little army had become.

As for the battle in the Mountain and Abu Ammar [Yasser Arafat's *nom de guerre*] the campaign was forced on him by the need to take the isolationists from behind, on their own terrain, and in confrontations which were infinitely less costly than those in Beirut. As one who knows the history and geography of my country well, I myself instigated this campaign, which was geared to shorten the war. Within two weeks, we seemed about to achieve our goal. The isolationists, taken by surprise, were hastily signalling their agreement to nearly all the points in our programme of political reform. We were awaiting their surrender and peace at Reyfoun or at Beit Mery. But the Syrians saw things differently. They wanted the bargaining, and hence their arbitration, to continue at all cost. It was a matter of narrow self-interest and prestige. The Syrian Army advanced in Chtaura, in Zahle, in Mderej, in Sofar, in Ouyoun el-Simane and in Akkar, with the clear aim of surrounding us. So much for their mission of charity.

Abu Ammar must have been fully aware of the risk he was taking.

I know . . . but we did not assess the risk very precisely. We were relying on Europe, on the United States, on France, on the Arabs and on the Syrians themselves to prevent President Assad sending in his army. We did not really believe in the danger of a military intervention, perhaps because we were not fully informed about the relations between Washington and Damascus or about the pressure that Washington was putting on Israel. In any case, we have no regrets. At least we have shown up the Syrian policy for what it is and exposed the aims of nearly all the so-called nationalist and progressive Arab governments. We have initiated a movement which may prove to be irreversible and which will permanently mark the evolution of the Arab world. I hope that we will shortly witness a return to the democratic institutions demanded by public opinion. Sadat has opened up the path to freedom, for all the attendant bitterness. Algeria and perhaps even Morocco seem inclined to follow suit.

We were the victim offered up as sacrifice on the altar of U.S. and Israeli interests. Certain Arab States played the role of scapegoat during the performance of this pointless ritual. The right has slipped the leash, supported and abetted by the progressive Ba'ath regime, and we are now suffering the consequences. But later, the nationalist reformist movement of the left will re-emerge and will be even stronger than in the past. Our aim is to turn our defeat into a future victory, whilst doing what we can to avoid frightening Islam and Arabism with the spectre of communism or any other social and political scarecrow.

Why is it so difficult to introduce democracy in Arab countries? Are there any special obstacles?

No. Syria, Iraq, Sudan, Kuwait and Egypt all used to have parliamentary regimes. On the whole, they operated on European lines. It was the formation of the State of Israel in 1948 and the failure of the Arab armies to cope with the fact of Israel's existence that triggered off a whole series of *coup d'etats* and revolutions in the Arab world. Personally, I attribute the lack of democracy in the Arab world to the fact that the ruling parties have proved incapable of mobilizing public opinion, and also to the preponderant role of the Army in certain regimes.

These supposedly progressive regimes, which in practice have so much in common with Franco's, undoubtedly only survive thanks to the tacit approval of various foreign powers. But given the way they manage their affairs, I think they cannot last for much longer. Changes are inevitable, either before or after Geneva: perhaps the Arab world needs some catalyst before it can begin to move towards forms of democracy. Under the Abbassid Caliphate, there was a period of almost complete freedom in the Arab empire; it lasted for nearly two hundred years. Then, I am not sure why, the curtain came down.

On the whole, I am not pessimistic about the future, because regimes are becoming more democratic — throughout the world, even in the Soviet Union and the communist countries. The intelligentsia must, in the long run, win back its rights, and the most important of those rights is freedom of expression, both scientific and political. I cannot believe that the Arab countries will be the exception to this rule. Even Syria will have to adapt.

So Islam is not an impediment to democracy?

On the contrary. A kind of democracy was preached and then established during the Prophet's lifetime, and during the reign of the first Caliphs, the Rachidines. It has often been said of Omar Ibn Khattab that he was a liberal leader who accepted criticism from many sources; many of the Caliphs of that period could be described as social democrats. Islam introduced a measure of social equality, especially in its initial phase, before people got richer and a capitalist class emerged.

Could France have played an important role in settling the conflict? She offered to intervene but her proposal was turned down. Fahmi, and later you yourself, went to Paris. It seemed then that France could help in some way, but in the end everything was decided in Riyadh.

France botched her chance to intervene in the Lebanese crisis. She was not patient enough to wait for the role which should have been hers and which would have won her universal support.

Giscard's France is not the France of Pompidou or de Gaulle. The U.S. is always lurking in the background. Throughout the Lebanese crisis, it was clear that France's policy had lost its independent character, both in Europe and in the Middle East. Reformists and technocrats are not necessarily statesmen. A politician takes decisions with a view to achieving a specific goal. A technocrat is more interested in how things are to be done. It was a pity that Paris remained so ambiguous and vague; after all, economic interests aside, France has a political position to defend in Europe and in the world. National policy is above all a matter of aims and principles: it cannot be managed like an insurance company. The General would have understood. But the French have become too rich, too susceptible to an American influence which ill befits Paris. Mediocrity and indifference to others is the order of the day.

Perhaps France can no longer afford to take an interest in the affairs of others.

I think she can. There are many countries with far fewer means at their disposal who still play a role in world affairs. One only has to think of Yugoslavia, of Nasser's Egypt, of India, Iran, Israel, etc. Here and there, little countries venture to tilt the balance of events, because they know how to interpret and represent their geo-political and cultural position. Economics is not everything. A united, 'nationalized' Lebanon committed to humanism, to developing and reasserting its culture in the context of Arabism could also play such a role.

After my journey to Paris, I thought France would send a delegation to Lebanon, or even troops in association with an Egyptian contingent, as President Sadat had proposed. I cannot say why France did nothing in the end. Perhaps because of American pressure, perhaps she was too busy with domestic and European problems; perhaps, also, because she is no longer Gaullist and no longer seeks to maintain her special relationship with

Lebanon and the Middle East. But there is still a role for France here. The telegram sent by M. de Guiringaud to Raymond Edde who had just escaped an assassination attempt was welcomed here as a sign of French interest. Why is Paris still so hesitant? Perhaps because of the nature of the present French government; it would seem that technocrats find it difficult to take real political decisions. As we see it, it is crucial that France retains a presence in Lebanon, and her friendship is particularly valuable to us.

M. de Guiringaud announced that he would only send the French Army into Lebanon once peace had been re-established. Well, now there is peace . . . . Only the influence of a great power, be it European or Arab, can really help us to maintain democracy in our country, to remain ourselves and safeguard our independence and our frontiers.

But France was repeatedly in contact with the Syrians, both before and after the major offensive. First Khaddam, and then Assad himself went to Paris.

I think the Syrian Government concentrated on misleading the French Government. Damascus feared that France would intervene before the Syrian Army had seized vast areas of Lebanon. Remember that Middle East politics is a tissue of lies and trickery. If France now decided to take a real interest in our country, Khaddam or Assad would be straight off to Paris again. In any case, there is still time for France to do something for Lebanon.

Yet when France, through its President, proposed to send troops to Lebanon, you rejected the offer vehemently, accusing her of 'vestigial colonialism'. And now you say that Europe must assert itself in the Middle East.

We never rejected a French political intervention. You are no doubt aware of our relations with M. Gorse and M. Couve de Murville. We would now welcome some form of French mediation. But the suggestion of a French military intervention in Lebanon was put forward during a speech given by President Giscard d'Estaing in the U.S., and we had reason to fear that, at the time, the proposal was the result of an agreement with the Americans and the C.I.A., who had been amongst the initiators of the plot against Lebanon. We dreaded that the French troops would come to join the Maronites — at a time when the Syrians were already in possession of at least half of our territories — thereby creating the impression that the partition of the country was a *fait accompli*. Had the circumstances been different, I can assure you that we would not have rejected a French military intervention; we know that the days of the Mandate are well and truly past and that France would now be an impartial arbiter.

I met M. Gorse in Paris, and he was unable to understand how you could have interpreted his offer in this way.

My reaction was over-hasty. I should have waited a few days before speaking. But we were so frightened of seeing our country cut in half, it was a defensive reflex. We would no doubt have had a different attitude towards the French proposal — especially as France intended to limit its intervention to the ports, certain public institutions, the airport, Jounie, etc. — had it not been announced in the United States.

Do you envisage any new alliances between factions which fought each other during the civil war but might eventually unite around a new objective?

We do not know what is the ultimate Syrian aim. Do they intend to treat the solution of the Lebanese problem as part and parcel of a broader solution, which would also encompass the Palestinian problem? Would that mean that they would accept the formation of an independent Maronite State? Personally, I doubt that they would go so far, but assuredly Israel will look unfavourably upon Syria's growing influence in Lebanon, and if the isolationists are genuinely loyal to their own idea of Lebanon, they will soon change their position. It remains to be seen how many of those on the other side, who now evince friendship towards Damascus, really expect this state of affairs to continue. Is the other side really willing to allow the old parliamentary democracy to be re-established in Lebanon? I am prepared to believe it, but first they will have to wake up to some political realities. President Sarkis is, I suspect, already beginning to realize what has to be done to save the country.

During the war, at least two of the progressive movements claimed allegiance to Nasser's ideals. You yourself have repeatedly referred to a 'genuine Nasserist ideology'. What exactly do you mean by that?

I think what I said was that Nasser had managed to develop an ideology that suited the Arab world, which was in no way excessive and yet breathed new life into all the myths of Arab nationalism. At one time, this ideology, and Nasser's image, dominated the spirit of the Arab masses. It has remained fixed in people's subconscious, which is why groups in Beirut, in Damascus, in Baghdad, just about everywhere, still invoke his memory. In Lebanon, several groups base themselves on his doctrine, that was both nationalist and socialist. The Arab nation, which has been so long misunderstood and has only recently begun to develop its self-awareness, refers to Nasser as a way of defining a meaning to life which is specific to itself; a political and social concept which draws certain fundamental social ideas from Marxism and socialism, yet does not turn its back on its own ethnic origins or on Islam. In Syria, in Libya and throughout the Arab world, Nasser is seen as the hero of this nationalist socialism. If he were still alive these movements would certainly have gained considerable influence over the destiny of the Arab countries.

Personally, I do not draw my inspiration either from Nasser or from

Nasserism; our movement dates back to 1947. But I do feel that Nasser was the founder of a rich and interesting body of ideas, especially when he preached what I would call a co-operative socialism which did not neglect the role of the spiritual. Had those ideas been applied fully, Egypt would have benefited greatly, for they represent a human and sincere socialism. Once the land reform and the reform of industrial management were complete, the next step should have been an attack on the structure of real estate ownership, so as to favour small and middle-sized holdings. Economic factors have prevented President Sadat from continuing with these policies and endowing this new form of socialism with a deeper, fairer and more realistic content. I feel that Nasser understood that small and middle-sized property ownership was historically progressive and a natural social development more in keeping with the order of things than communal ownership; he realized that socialism is not necessarily collectivism. Marx's interpreters and followers have not yet grasped this ultimately progressive and natural character of small-scale or co-operative ownership.

Could the Lebanese crisis have repercussions as important for the Arab world as Nasser's conceptions?

I cannot say, but I believe that if, despite all the obstacles, democracy is re-established and strengthened, the Arab world will be profoundly changed as a result — in the medium and long term at least. In any case, liberty is increasingly in the air since President Sadat began to install some form of democratic regime in Egypt. Algeria will, I think, follow suit: she has already endowed herself with a Constitution, established public institutions and proclaimed the rule of law. I cannot believe that Syria will not eventually adopt a similar course. Libya is already firmly committed to direct democracy, thanks to President Ghadaffi's initiatives. In the long run, democracy must surely be restored throughout the Arab world, in response to the craving for freedom of all these Mediterranean peoples. There is a certain stubborn and deep-seated Bedouin love of democracy, which is both spontaneous and specific to the Arabs. Of course, one cannot discount the danger that the people will become accustomed to being deprived of freedom and end up by finding the lack of it quite natural (as in the communist countries or under military dictatorships). But it would seem that in many communist countries, in the Soviet Union and elsewhere, individual, social and political freedom is already on the horizon. Some of my communist friends believe that, by 1985, democracy will have made considerable progress in most of the Eastern Bloc. Socialism without freedom is not socialism: it is blighted by an alienation of the spirit.

There are still hundreds of thousands of guns in Lebanon. Is this just an armed truce or would you agree to hand over your heavy weapons and your stocks of ammunition?

We would find it difficult to turn our weapons over to anybody, firstly because we, the population, paid for them ourselves, and secondly because the other side finds it far easier to hide its weapons and to obtain new ones. All the churches (there are 2,000 of them in Lebanon) are prepared to serve as secret storehouses, as are the barracks of the official forces and the Maronites, the monasteries and the convents. It is no easy matter for Arab troops to go and search such places. The isolationists thus have at their disposal ample means to move their weapons from one hideout to another at will. We do not. We will therefore have to wait until the constitutional reform has been accepted by everybody before we will no longer need our weapons. The reform will have to be based on the great principles of political renewal proposed by the various parties, and the elimination of political confessionalism.

So the region will remain a powderkeg?

No, I do not think so, providing the Arab troops maintain a clear line of demarcation. The full reaction to the entry of the Syrian Army into the Maronite areas is yet to come. It will undoubtedly disillusion all those who sought to create a State for the so-called Maronite nation, all those who wanted partition, especially President Shamun. The isolationists refused to admit that Lebanon was Arab, and now Arab troops, Bedouin included, have invaded their territory, set up camp there and enforced the law. They wanted an independent or semi-independent administration; now they have no such option. All their projects have come to nothing, even regionalism. A backlash is inevitable and all the true Christian leaders, the real patriots like Raymond Edde, will be rewarded for what they suffered during the war at the hands of the pseudo-Christians on the other side. There will have to be a major dialogue between the Maronite rank and file and their leaders, civil and military. These leaders will obviously not emerge from such a debate with any credit. What can they tell their people? Nothing.

In fact, Raymond Edde seems more displeased by the arrival of the Syrian troops than Camille Shamun.

Perhaps because he realizes that the Lebanese State is still too weak to ask the Syrians to go home. It is not an unacceptable point of view. The fact that the Syrian troops are here as participants in an Arab action, with unanimous Arab consent, gives one reasonable grounds for believing that these troops will not stay here if President Sarkis takes an immediate initiative to reorganize the army, and especially the internal security forces. The moment these forces have grown to 10,000 to 12,000 men, they will be able to maintain order on their own, provided they are properly equipped. The Syrians will then have to leave.

Do you feel that peace is on the way and might be achieved within a year or 18 months, or do you think that the various rejection fronts — Israeli, Palestinian and others — will prevail over whatever tentative moves towards a settlement Washington might make?

The way I see it is that everybody is running towards Geneva, everybody wants to sit around the conference table. The question is whether, in the meantime, the governments which are seemingly willing to accept a partial solution to the Palestinian problem will be able to continue on such a course. They certainly will not be able to do so if a front of Arab States hostile to any partial solution is formed. In the Middle East, one always has to take into account the possibility of a change of regime, but the way things are going, Geneva just might succeed.

In which case the real issue is as follows: will the 1,200,000 Palestinian refugees, who would be reduced to a diaspora and who will number 2 or 3 million ten years hence, accept their fate? A great deal depends on the attitude of Yasser Arafat and the P.L.O. Will they be able to remain as flexible as they are now if they are not given a guarantee that their little State will not be integrated into some Syrian-Jordanian confederation, which could easily become much more firmly united following a *coup d'etat* or some new agreement, and which would thereby represent a far more serious threat to the Hebrew State than the — at present — divided countries of the Levant? In the last analysis, everything depends on the Soviets and the Americans; there seems to be some measure of agreement between them as to the content of a Geneva solution.

How do you envisage the Arab world 20 years from now?

That is a very difficult question to answer. I fear that it will become too westernized, in the bad sense, too dependent on the machine and its various forms of psychic, physical, ecological and moral alienation. Man is a great mimic — a true descendant of the monkeys — and this is particularly true of us Semites. Often, one has to go as far as one can with a materialist civilization before one can understand its consequences, its deformities, its elementary deficiencies. A flaw may be staring you in the face, yet you will not necessarily notice it. The power of illusion, *maya,* dominates you and carries you along. And when these flaws, these deformities, these deficiencies reach their peak, it is often too late to go back. Moral intoxication prevails, the cycle of decomposition begins and nothing can be done about it. The people as a whole are powerless to intervene, despite all the theories of popular consciousness and sovereignty, the ideal of a far-seeing democracy. The whole world is threatened by mechanization. Call it a machination if you like . . . .

Nonetheless, I feel that a great social revolution or change is sweeping from country to country throughout the Arab world; there is also a far greater psychological understanding of the problems of tomorrow. The form of socialism which is emerging promises to be something new. Even the over-rich oil states will not be able to avoid it. Arab nationalism will continue to develop, despite the present difficulties, and there will be a steady move towards Arab unity, between several peoples if not between all. But I fear that the sword will play its part in this process of unification. Islam will, as always, bind people together. It will have to return to its sources as well as undergo a regeneration. One cannot avoid the fact that, without Islam, the Arabs would have no cohesion. In fact, as Ibn Khaldun so rightly pointed out, the Arab nation needs a sustained emotional driving force, a degree of fanaticism (*assabiya*). Perhaps this applies to all peoples, but it is particularly true of the Arab Semites.

In the meantime, the population will have continued to grow, we will be a nation of 300 to 400 million souls. Europe and the world should take warning; Israel is a problem which was created quite senselessly, against the wishes of the Arabs and in flagrant contradiction to natural justice — you cannot just take away a people's country and give it to another in the middle of the 20th Century. This problem, if it is not resolved, will be the leaven, the detonator that will ignite the Arab world and animate its will to power and its fully justified sense of grievance.

A similar wave of unrest is coursing throughout the world. We are at the dawn of a new era, an apocalyptic period. Will this Orient, where God's spirit seems to haunt the valleys, the mountains and the deserts, witness the birth of He whose coming is foretold by nearly all the esoteric doctrines of the world, the Founder of the Universal Religion, or at least of an all-embracing doctrine which will replace the sectarianisms of today? What is certain is that, just about everywhere, people are searching for a new philosophical, religious and scientific gnosticism. The present state of divorce from the spirit cannot last much longer.

If I have one hope, it is that the Arab Union will once again be able to progress towards that free and human communion of Arab peoples, organized in a Commonwealth, a collectivity of mullahs, as in the days of the Arab Caliphate or the Turkish Sultanate; in other words, a synergy of peoples, cultures and forces, of which freedom will surely be one element.

Reform in Lebanon will unfortunately have to wait for a good while, until Geneva is first convened and then either succeeds or fails. How do you define your responsibilities to those whom you led into battle and who must now be so frustrated?

Human stupidity always intervenes in our affairs, as do personal questions — the ego makes history — and all too often our enterprises break down, leaving us misunderstood and scorned. Another factor is a people's *karma,* the habits acquired from a civilization, the classifications supposedly civilized men impose upon themselves. The human cycle has many downturns.

But one has to do one's duty, and once the furrow has been ploughed, it too becomes a latent or directly causal factor. Sometimes the path is more important than the immediate result. One simply has to go on, digging a deeper furrow.

And let us not forget that men are, by their very nature, eternally frustrated. They enjoy momentary satisfactions, a temporary quenching of their thirst; then the quest begins again. So much the better, for otherwise men would become too bourgeois, in the strict, class-free sense of the word. It is this driving force which pushes new ideologies and doctrines to the fore, in the constant process by which history is simultaneously given value and falsified.

I have to say that the programme of democratic reforms we have proposed is based on a fairminded conception. We did not just listen to what people had to say — though we naturally took their counsel into account — we also sought the Good, the Real, the Harmonious and the Just, not allow-- ing ourselves to be diverted by any considerations of self-interest or demagogy. We wanted to discover the inner law which governs all true democracies, drawing on the historical experience of all peoples, but also on the conception of good government itself. We had no intention of slavishly pursuing a notion of popular sovereignty where there is, strictly speaking, no sovereignty to be had. For us, the essential problem was that of the elite which would emerge from the social group. We wanted to draw forth the real elite, the truest form of elite. And we were concerned to map what one might call the social functions, the interconnections of that organism which is the nation and society.

For us, justice is that which, at a given moment, genuinely reflects or expresses the inherent relationship between an institution and its function. In other words, justice demands a definition of human motives, a set of moral purposes rather than a mess of slogans and an empty liberalism which can be as oppressive and destructive as dictatorship itself.

Such a programme of reforms will attract all those who are looking for an alternative to the incomplete democracy of the old nations of Europe and to the totalitarian regimes of right and left which have robbed man of his historical liberation from the collective.

We have no wish to entrust our fate to an absolute liberalism, blindly seeking its own path and the laws of its development. We want to develop a scientific analysis of the body politic, as a perennial entity, in order to bring to light the specifically human and beneficial motivations within it, the internal and external laws of their *dharma,* within the context of mankind's real destiny. One cannot simply leave everything to the whims and passions of individuals, to the vagaries of new scientific discoveries or to the ambitions of the technocrats. I feel that the old concepts of Roman Law and the not dissimilar ideas of the Hindu *Sanatana Dharma* have a great deal to teach us in this respect. It is so often by means of a return to one's sources that one rejuvenates oneself and initiates a renaissance. This is the perspective within which we in the Progressive Socialist Party have envisaged and developed our ideas on politics, society, the economy and civilization.

Perhaps one day, when the times are more propitious, I will try to express all this in another book. As Teilhard de Chardin says, 'The important thing about any effort is to "see".'

In Lebanon, everybody describes you as 'an old fox when it comes to politics'. Yet during this crisis, you have not acted as a political fox but rather as a committed individual, perhaps even an adventurer. How do you account for your reputation and your commitment during the course of this war?

People call others what they choose, because they are used to seeing others only as a form, an idea, and a name. Furthermore, they attribute to others the qualities, the faults and the nicknames they themselves possess. It is a kind of unconscious 'reflexivity', like a mirror. Some individuals, some peoples even, also attribute to others the best in themselves, or see themselves in others as they would like to be. Idols are often created in this way. Of course, people can easily change from one point of view to another . . . look at Caesar and Brutus.

To tell the truth there is a bit of the fox, a bit of the adventurer and a bit of the committed man in all of us. In any case, commitment entails adventure, for good or ill. And is not intelligence itself a fox?

Any action is always a mixture of commitment and compromise. Life is made up of an infinite multitude of compromises. The person who does not know how to compromise does not know how to act. But compromise is not surrender of one's principles. Ghandi put it very well when he said, 'Love of truth has taught me the beauty of compromise.' Also, you must always think of your people and constantly make sure that they are behind you. You are working for them, after all, not for yourself. In practice, one is often acting in one's own interest, but the mask must constantly be torn away and any imposture exposed if one is to achieve that inner peace and detachment which comes from not being guided by ambition or pleasure.

But the others, those on whose behalf you claim to act, those whom you seek to guide often need rest, a way station on the climbing road. 'The spirit is willing but the flesh is weak.' That is why one should never indulge in political Quixoticism, be it Hitlerism, Stalinism or any of the other games for Caesars and Popes. Personally I prefer a true Quixoticism, an attitude to human action which is always a little self-critical. One should not take oneself too seriously, even when one is being as serious as possible in one's actions. In life, one is always tilting at windmills and a sense of humour is essential if one is not to become vain and superficial. Honour and purity are always worth preserving.

The crucial thing is to be honest, or, if you will permit me a Hindu turn of phrase, to maintain a spirit of authenticity. And nothing can be more authentic than to fulfil one's own *dharma* (I like the word *dharma*, which means the 'path-duty-destiny' which has been allotted to each of us). It is quite useless to pursue any *dharma* except your own. If only everybody realized that there would be so much less misery, unsatisfied desire and frustrated ambition in the world. In practice, I have always been both committed and free.

There can be no finer adventure than to chase after Truth, to pursue the True, the Just, harmony and moderation in all things. Once again, 'love of truth' — in whatever form — has taught me the 'beauty of compromise'.

The events in Lebanon called for total commitment. We had to wade through the sewer which lay before us; all the ignoble bastardly activity which goes with a revolution which was badly managed, badly led right from the start — and there was so much dirty work being done, the licentiousness of disoriented youth, the Bedouin anarchy of the Arabs, the violence and passion which characterizes this cycle of civilization. It was practically impossible to clean these Augean stables. But it had to be done, it was worth doing. And therein lies the basis for our first self-criticism.

Instead of contenting ourselves with restraining the worst excesses, we should perhaps have sought to control this infernal and heroic trudge through the mire, in order to prevent it becoming either a Paris Commune or a Spanish Civil War. The presence of the Palestinians, the multiplicity of parties and groups involved, the delay in creating a civil authority, the need to bring everybody together in a broad front in order to stand up to a powerful enemy, all made the task seem so far beyond our capacities.

And then there was a personal problem. In 33 years of political struggle, one's idealism softens. Weariness and the sense of tilting at windmills were sapping my morale. In my case, too, 'the spirit was willing but the flesh was weak'.

I kept thinking of what a great sage had said: 'You will never change the world. All you can do is to change yourself. But once you get there, you will see that everything is in its proper place, everything is as it should be.' To change the world is, above all, to change people. Yet nearly all the great human adventures have failed. But *dharma* is *dharma,* one has to go on, fulfilling duty itself rather than simply one's own duty.

There was another reason for extreme commitment during the 1975-76 events in Lebanon. It would have been wrong to break the psychological stride of our young people, who were finally beginning to move. The ideological and emotional cycle which was driving them on had to be completed. These young people imbued with revolutionary socialism, with Marxism, with Leninism, Maoism and Guevarism, with Fascism and Falangism, with Ba'athism and all the other noisy 'isms' of the subconscious, needed to go all the way along the path of revolutionary involvement, rather than stop at the very beginning of the road, as happened in 1968 in France.

I feel confident that Lebanese youth will emerge from this dirty and heroic struggle much wiser, much more mature, much readier to carry out a real revolution rather than mere revolutionary gestures. A revolutionary worthy of the name — that is to say one who behaves with the moral purity and sense of honour which befits the task before him — is a creative artisan who brings joy to the world. Morality and revolution go hand in hand. The objectives and motives of a revolution always depend on the moral conscience of both the leaders and the people as much as on the historical causality defined by historical materialism. It is the distinctive feature of man never to act blindly, without the illumination of some interior light, even — and in fact especially — if he is a sincere atheist.

It is the moral purpose which counts . . . . All the demographic, economic, social, technical and cultural factors take this intentionality, this moral *sanalpa* as their fulcrum. Man is above all a moral thing, the deepseated aim of his life is to fulfil himself within his generic concept of mankind. Everything in him strains towards transcendence, whatever those I call the false witnesses may say to the contrary, be they materialists, or Christians or Muslims.

In the end, our political strategy demanded that we push the other side, the isolationists, into a cul-de-sac — the impasse from which the Syrian intervention has briefly rescued them. I say briefly, because now they will have to face the accusations of the population and the young people they have betrayed.

Could you sum up the main points of your self-criticism? How would you define the mistakes you made?

What I have just said, constitutes the beginnings of a self-criticism. We were, for a while, a little too idealistic. We felt that it was imperative not to let our young people come to a halt when we began to feel the obstacles mounting up before us. We did not want a May 1968, we did not want all those who aspired to social change to feel we had let them down the moment things became difficult.

It was vital that they share in that moral rectitude, that intransigent loyalty which makes for untroubled consciences; the knowledge that one has done one's duty. We were intensely aware that we had come to an historical turning-point in the country's social and political life. We had to take this historical opportunity to raise people's consciousness to a new level on a lasting basis. We were like a man who is climbing towards the peak of a mountain and then is forced to turn back by the wind, the incipient storm and the clouds which are covering up the landscape. The evocative power of the magnificent panorama he has glimpsed will stay with him. One should not forget that peoples have memories too, and that their collective subconscious plays a crucial role in the realization of political and social goals. And we had to offer some gleam of hope, some vision of the promised tomorrow. To live through such an existential experience — E. Cioran describes it as a plunge into existence — purifies and invigorates, in that it offers a glimpse of the future one is trying to build. The imagination of peoples, like that of individuals, plays an important role in all real activity, and it needs must have some ideal summit to aim for, however clouded over.

When the Syrian troops poured in from the east, when it became clear that the United States had given them the green light and that we had been abandoned by almost everybody, we felt that, despite our political failure, our rejection by the Arabs and by Damascus, it was vital to prepare the Arab and Lebanese masses to take control of their own future. We were and still are convinced that we were fighting for everybody, for all the Arabs, and that the political regimes that have imprisoned and dispossessed their peoples will not be able to hold back the dawn much longer.

To return to our self-criticism we entertained a great many illusions about the attitude of the Arab peoples and the regimes that govern them. We were fighting for everybody, on everybody's behalf, but the Arabs seemed determined to ignore the fact. Most of the regimes seemed intent on preventing their peoples from supporting, let alone following us. The regimes did everything they could to misinform their peoples. The bourgeois who lurks just below the surface of these Arab leaders had no wish to have his petty political projects disturbed by our little adventure.

Most Arab politicians, and sometimes the Arab people themselves, lack that sense of human possibility which makes for the greatness of our destiny. They are only provincial *walis,* as in the final days of the fictitious Caliphates of Baghdad or Cairo. The idea of the State in the modern or Graeco-Roman sense is nearly always absent from their preoccupations. Most of these 'progressive' regimes are a clumsy, distorted and ugly copy of the communist regimes on the one hand, the military dictatorships of Latin America on the other: the one-party state, the single legitimate ideology, the intelligence services, the contempt for human rights and civil liberty, the repressive structure of political activity, the empty slogans, the absence of any genuine revolutionary spirit — as in most of the present-day communist regimes, incidentally — the lack of any genuinely revolutionary thought — it all adds up. As for the regimes which are more usually referred to as reactionary, they are even worse; the prince or the rulers treat the State and its revenues as their own property.

Of course, we did have Nasser, but he came and went like a tornado, a meteor. The Arab peoples all felt the impact and saw the flash of promise, but even if they all applauded, they did not necessarily all follow. This world of seraglios and sand, of mosques, traditions, and nationalism, rich in oil, agriculture and money needs a leader — a new enlightened leader, a Frederick II, a Peter the Great or a Bismarck. If he whom Arnold Toynbee called 'the Arab Bismarck' failed in his task, it is because Arab tribalism, the narrowmindedness of the *walis,* with their petty provincialism, prevailed.

And now we are threatened by what I would call an economic and political Americanization, that degenerate form of the old pragmatism which at least had the merit of referring to certain basic values quite frequently. Americanism may be good for America but it is a poisonous export. The European peoples are losing their souls to it.

No people or empire has ever had at its disposal financial wealth and energy resources comparable to those of the Arabs today, and never has a people or an empire shown itself so incapable of putting what it had to good use.

We were amazed at the Syrian regime's *volte-face.* It seemed the epitome of illogicality. We expected more consistency, more reserve, more tact and more principles from them. It is now all in the past, but it completely upset our calculations. As I often say to some of my Marxist friends: in the Arab world, no single dialectic can be correctly applied. The Marxist-Leninist dialectic, the dialectic of constraints, must be profoundly revised, reformed and extended if it is to analyse and assess events in the Arab countries, where the illogical and the irrational rule. Every dialectic must be adapted to the period and the peoples concerned; its essence may still be valid, but in its application it must take on a local coloration in response to the facts of experience, it must be made relative to a particular time, place and set of circumstances.

Another mistake we made — a fatal one, as it happened — was not to organize ourselves into an efficient civil administration sooner. It was an immense task, given the presence of the various divergent Palestinian organizations (especially in Beirut) and also because of the multitude of left parties and groups, each with their secret antagonisms, their craving for a place in the limelight, and all too often their complete lack of political experience. There was no overall plan, no generally accepted ruling party, no real integration — it was almost a *cour des miracles*. We should have made the tremendous effort required to bring order to this chaos. Perhaps we lacked the will, perhaps we felt the whole thing was, in any case, too precarious. To build up an organization would have meant concentrating on the overall picture and the individual details simultaneously, and would have required a very methodical approach, without which nothing ever comes to anything in the East.

Another failing was our inability to interest the people in our economic and social reforms. We could have done so before the Syrians arrived. Well, that was my opinion anyway. The big estates of Akkar, the Bekaa, the South and Mount Lebanon could have been broken up and redistributed and then we could have proceeded to share out the urban properties amongst the tenants on a floor by floor basis. Another reform I am particularly attached to is the idea of fair rents for apartments. These should be fixed at 8 to 10% of the building cost of the property, excluding the cost of the land it stands on. That is what I call a fair price. Shopkeepers' rents could also be fixed, at 15 to 30%, according to location. This system would enable us to cut price, income and rent inflation drastically. We should have implemented other reforms as well, to present the new Arab Lebanon with a *fait accompli*. Such reforms might even have attenuated if not deferred the Syrian intervention itself. And we would have attracted far wider and stronger popular support as a result.

We needed an organization to carry these tasks through. As it was, the activities of the various parties, all striving to attract new members, degenerated into a free for all, an anarchy of opportunism as in Allende's Chile. Whenever one creates a party, especially if it is based on a closed ideology, the result is usually a new church. Parties have few worse enemies than their own members. Incidentally, one of our friends from the communist labour organization pointed out that a reform of the rent system and the imposition of fair prices for leases would have alienated nearly all the citizens of Beirut, the overwhelming majority of whom are landlords rather than tenants. Paradoxes abound in this city of a thousand facets!

Another mistake, and not the least of them, was that certain Marxist parties were too prominent in our Central Political Council. We had not reckoned with the sordid use the Lebanese right and our Syrian friends might make of the fact. It was not long before an anti-communist hue and cry began. And we had not appreciated just how anti-communist and undiscerning Islam could be in its attitudes and judgements.

Other failings one might add to this list include the dogmatic anti-Americanism of certain nationalist and Marxist movements. People can be drugged into a stupor by ideology, as a result of which they become blind to subtle distinctions; in particular, there was very little understanding of the original features and internal dynamic of the American experience. There are still people who will analyse facts and issue a prognosis exactly as a Marxist of 150 years ago might have done. These attitudes, violently expressed in the various journals, sometimes hampered our political initiatives, and we were often forced to correct them publicly, at a time when we needed everybody's support to save Lebanon's unity and democracy.

Other movements chose the very moment when the assassin's blade was at our throat to vent their spite on this or that Arab regime. The allegiances these parties owed often meant that they were neither independent nor perspicacious.

We also had reason to regret the chaos created by the Palestinians and nearly all the other parties, the tendency to unbridled self-indulgence and looting. It still amazes me how disappointingly immature and callow the young people turned out to be in this respect, for all their heroism, their commitment and their honesty. The young people treated the battle as a game, they threw themselves into it wholeheartedly, as if it were a sport. But as far as public and private property was concerned, they often behaved like migrating nomads or Bohemians. They had been perverted by ideology and the poor education they must have received from their families and schools. Stealing a car was known as 'pulling a car'. Stealing a house or a carpet was called 'requisitioning'. The problem with poorly understood Left ideologies is that they can provide an excuse for just about every one of man's cardinal sins. It was utterly disgusting; we felt they were dragging us all into the mire with them. We should have reacted more vehemently. We did try, but we also needed these strange kids aching to do battle. And I admit that, despite their misdeeds, I liked them a great deal. At least they were not hypocrites. But the wound has to be healed if what is best in our society is not to be destroyed.

We also had reason to regret the poor organization, and sometimes the poor leadership of the battles themselves, especially at the beginning. The Palestinians, too, must be reassessing their tactics. It was sometimes almost as if rival hordes were attacking each other. There was very little concern with pulling together and coherence, with adequate preparation and timing. There was nothing approaching European levels of co-ordination. Had it not been for this disorder, the fighting might have lasted for only half as long.

Furthermore, there was what I call the 'minuet' imposed at the end of each joust by the Syrians and the Palestinians: advance, return, advance, return, everytime the national and Palestinian forces had broken through the enemy lines. They seemed to treat the war as a series of sporting events. In the second stage of the struggle, once the isolationists had been given time to regroup their forces, they attacked again and our forces had to pay the same price in blood and effort all over again, to win back each street, each building which had slipped through our hands in the course of the peace negotiations. Every time we won the slightest victory, the isolationists (and especially the Falangists, who, like President Frangie, had established close relations with Damascus over the previous two or three years) would cry for help and appeal to the successive Syrian governments. The latter, ever ready to respond, would then set off for Beirut – at the instigation of President Assad – to separate the combatants and to compel the national and Palestinian forces to withdraw from the positions they had conquered. Our protests were all in vain. At the time, we had no heavy weapons with which to hold the terrain.

Delivery of our weapons and munitions stockpiled in Syria was tightly controlled and we were systematically denied access to heavy weapons, thereby making us dependent upon the Palestinians who, in turn, acted in concert with the Syrians. Nearly all the heavy weapons we purchased, and those sent to us by certain Arab States are still kept under heavy guard in Syria, along with an immense quantity of light weapons. Furthermore, the weapons we were supposed to receive were often requisitioned by our Palestinian friends and allies in Fatah while in transit through Lebanon. These 'confiscations' were always carried out secretly and without warning. Each time the theft was revealed, a thousand excuses were proffered, but the shipments never arrived for all that, or at least never arrived intact. There was a sort of tacit understanding between the Syrian Ba'ath, certain senior Palestinian leaders, and perhaps some others: firstly, never to allow the Socialist Party to become a real military force and an indepen-dent or determinant element in the war; secondly, never to supply the parties allied to us, especially the left parties, with sufficient weapons to become militarily effective.

And yet our ill-equipped, sometimes even ill-trained forces struggled with remarkable energy. People from all the various parties fought against odds of five or even ten to one, and managed to push back the enemy – forced them to retreat and seized some of their arms and munitions as our forces advanced into the terrain we had conquered.

The isolationists, despite their long training both at home and abroad, their many commando groups, their superior armament, their tanks, their armoured vehicles and their cannons, their ferocity, sharpened as it was by the American-inspired bloodbath approach to training, were constantly defeated, for all their 'crusader' fanaticism. They were good assassins when the need arose, but rather poor soldiers. It was only thanks to their near-perfect organization that they were at all effective.

Whenever heavy weapons came on the market, we hastened to purchase some. But our Palestinian allies usually outbid us. The Progressive Socialist Party and I myself had less to complain about in this respect than the other parties. At least we managed to get some of the arms we were due to receive. But for the others, it was a real ordeal. The whole war was run like a caravan-serai. We and our allies in the parties tried to bring some order into it but it was fruitless. Petty anarchy, which seems to be an intrinsic feature of the Arab character, invariably prevailed.

Our idealism, our loyalty towards the young people and the Palestinians, forced us to continue the struggle until we had won a decisive victory. The evidence of large-scale destruction forced us to seek the most rapid con-clusion to the hostilities, as did an ever-present concern at the mass murders perpetrated by the isolationists upon the civilian population, followed by the dynamiting of their houses and the imposition of an exodus. Again and again, I told the Syrians and the Palestinians: 'For God's sake, either commit your-selves sufficiently to put an end to the whole business, or else force Mr. Frangie and the Falangists to accept an agreement and stop this atrocious war, this purgatory.'

Of course, the Palestinians had their own problems in terms of arms and munitions supplies, or at least so they claimed. But it was as if everybody was agreed not to allow the National Movement to triumph or even to win a decisive battle. Damascus kept us under its benevolent eye, the telephone rang ten times a week, political arbitration was offered and then imposed. Egypt itself appealed to Pierre Gemayel's patriotism and commonsense. The Saudis, the Kuwaitis and others all urged us to be compassionate and prudent; apparently, they cared nothing for the fate of Arabism, of the nationalist Christians or of the Muslims of Lebanon. We did what we could to convince them of the obvious justice of our cause, but they nearly always accepted our opponents' point of view. Above all, they were terrified of communism. But even without this tiny communist fly in the ointment, they would still have been frightened. The *status quo* in Lebanon was some sort of guarantee as far as they were concerned; a guarantee of what, I have not the faintest idea.

An honest and patriotic minister of the Gulf States once asked our socialist comrade, Abbas Khalaf, who was on a mission to the area, 'What on earth are you after in Lebanon? You demanded democracy, but surely you must know that none of the Arab States want anything to do with it? You demand the abolition of confessional privileges, but nearly all the Arab States base themselves on a religious or confessional status. You propose a secularization of the laws and State institutions, which is anathema to everybody in the area. And yet, despite everything, you still ask for the moral and political support of the Arab States!'

Perhaps our mistake was not to have understood all this in time, or to have refused to understand it. I will pass over other mistakes we made, the list is endless. But nonetheless, we resisted; and morally, we feel that we triumphed, at least over ourselves.

At one point, we controlled 82% of the Lebanese territory and nearly all the towns. But just as the garrisons began to come over to our side, especially the one in Hammena with its heavy weapons and munitions; when the isolationists were just about to raise the white flag; when we held big villages such as Hrajel, Reyfoun in Kesruan, villages in the Metn such as Biskinta Chouein or Beit Mery; when even the people of Bikfaya wanted peace, the Syrians chose to send a regiment with 200 tanks to Masnaa to penetrate our territory, in response to President Frangie's desperate appeals. It was precisely during that period that Dean Brown, President Ford's special envoy, was in Beirut, perhaps to short-circuit the Lebanese mission mounted by Messrs Couve de Murville and Gorse and the possibility of a French intervention. That would have been typical of the Americans.

When I met Mr. Brown, who seemed so understanding of our problems in Lebanon, I could not help smiling at the parallel between his mission and that of the Turkish Minister, Fuad Pasha, sent to Lebanon by the Sublime Porte in 1860. I confess that, despite what was said in the papers and by nationalist and communist propaganda, our meeting with Mr. Brown proved reasonably fruitful. He was good enough to take note of our recommendation that the Chamber of Deputies be reconvened in order to amend the Constitution and hasten the election of a new President of the Lebanese Republic.

As I recall, the Saika and the Deputies loyal to Frangie and Shamun were opposed to the Chamber being reconvened. They threatened to bombard any eventual meeting place. Communications were opened with Frangie and Shamun, who were forced to climb down. The next step was to neutralize the Saika's opposition; President Ford sent a message on the subject to President Assad. The Chamber met and the proposals for the amendments to the Constitution were passed with an overwhelming majority. I then asked for a similar intervention concerning a meeting of the Chamber to organize the election of a new President. It took place as requested. At least the unity of the Lebanese State was preserved, whoever Mr. Frangie's successor might be. One cannot underestimate how much the Syrians were committed to their man, the ex-President. They even frequently told us that it was possible that his mandate would be renewed.

Obviously, we were always eager to talk with the representatives of the Soviet Union, France and various Arab countries — Egypt, Saudi Arabia, Iraq, Algeria, Kuwait, Libya, Tunisia, Morocco, Sudan — about these problems and initiatives, as well as with the P.L.O. and all our friends in the other Palestinian organizations. It was also important to prevent further penetration into Lebanon by the Syrian Army, and the attendant consequences. The Soviets exercised effective secret pressures on the Syrians in this respect, without breaking the ties of friendship uniting Damascus and Moscow however — or at least that is what the leaders of the great socialist nation assumed; our own assessment was somewhat different. Amidst all the confusion we felt that, slowly but surely, the Soviet attitude was hardening. Naturally, time was of the essence, hence our frequent impatience and anxiety.

Another mistake we made, in this Arab-Muslim world where almost no dialectical analysis really works, was our excessive reliance on the possibility that most of the Arab States would finally become less indifferent towards us, more concerned with our case. We continued to hope, but nothing happened. What a hall of mirrors this Arab world. There were times when public opinion in Europe was far more supportive than most of our Arab brothers. As for progressiveness . . . .

A further mistake was to have believed that Europe, or certain European nations at least, would intervene politically in our favour. We overlooked the determination of the two super-powers to keep the Arab Middle East as their private hunting ground. Our foreign contacts, our propaganda efforts in the outside world, even in the Arab world, were poorly organized. Our opponents were much better equipped and much more efficient in this area, right from the start.

In Beirut, especially, we had to take great care never to offend all those traditional Islamic leaders who have never understood anything about the Lebanese question, whose minds are stuck in the past of 25 years ago, who never do anything, who are quite incapable of leading but too selfish and vain to make way for more competent leaders. They waffle endlessly, regroup, separate again, constantly chattering like the old women in the Sursock quarter. Their notions of politics are rudimentary and crude, and they have almost no ideas about the reform of the State and the Constitution – indeed they shun such ideas, because the reform would go against their interests. And these 'personalities' were always noisily verbose: 'Why cannot Kamal Joumblatt and the Progressive Socialist Party carry the war up there, above Beirut? Their intervention would be decisive and there would be an end to this dirty war and to the bombardment of the city.' The traditional Shiite leaders, or some of them at least, also mumbled similar nonsense, at the very moment when hundreds of our comrades were fighting on several fronts in Beirut, in Tripoli, in Zahle, in Dannige, etc. And in fact we were eventually able to dominate three major *cazas,* the Chouf, Aley, the Upper Metn and nearly half of Mount Lebanon without firing a shot, simply by developing a strategy based on political, military and moral prestige. Beirut was saved from being surrounded. But the old women continued to natter.

As the war dragged on, it became imperative to take action, to defend the human rights of the Lebanese people. We were forced to launch the 'War for the Mountain' prematurely, before we were fully prepared, in other words before we had received even half of the weapons and munitions stock-piled on our behalf in Syria. Two weeks later we could have gone to war on a much better footing, better equipped, with better supplies; we could have won the decisive battle before the Syrian military intervention – which I have to admit we had never foreseen. Just as we had never foreseen that Syria would cut off our supplies of arms and munitions – 'our' arms and 'our' munitions.

Finally, I must confess, that sickened as I was by this sewer of daily violence, by the bloody massacres, by the endless twists and turns of Arab politics, and not being myself in command of the principal force in the area

(that prerogative remained the P.L.O.'s), I did not work as hard as I might
have done on the organization of the struggle, either on the military or the
civilian level. There were so many parties and groups, each with their own
set of allegiances to the Fatah or to other Palestinian organizations. Partisan
feelings of terrible pettiness were constantly coming to the surface. It was
chaos. And I admit, I myself often acted like a dilettante.

*You are the leader of an armed progressive movement which, during the
recent events, bombarded the other side daily and was, in its turn, constantly
under heavy fire. There has been a great deal of killing. What do you think
of violence in politics? In the specific case of Lebanon, is it not the most
obvious sign of a sad lack of imagination?*

I dislike violence. Those around me know my veneration for Ghandi. I
believe he is the true prophet of the modern age, for he reintroduced morality
into politics, at a time when the politicians, of West and East alike, sought to
shut it out. But I also believe that when one has an ideal and that ideal is
seriously in danger, when the choice is between submission and violence, then
one must opt for violence.

But most of the time there are other means available . . . .

One is often forced to use armed violence to save men, to save a country,
and because one has no other choice.

Does that not concern you?

I live for my ideal, you know. And remember Krishna, who was violent and
non-violent simultaneously.

*It is difficult to grasp the situation here. One feels it is as if violence were
somehow institutionalized.*

We managed to avoid violence for 12 months, by being firm, but in the
end there were those on the other side who were too intoxicated with the
crusader spirit, and who had been so for 20 or 30 years.

*Do you personally feel that you narrowly missed a great national and
Arab destiny?*

It may well be. If we had succeeded in Lebanon, it would have provoked a
wave of change throughout the Arab world. At the very least, we would have
stabilized and extended our system of political democracy, thereby opening
up the way for hitherto almost unimaginable social and economic evolution.
The left would have been restructured and improved as a result, by moving
in the opposite direction to all these dictatorial regimes that prevail here

and there throughout the world and especially in the Arab world. The Arabs need the window of freedom to be opened up for them: they are suffocating under the existing regimes which have mistakenly chosen to copy the out-dated structures and false concepts of communist democracy. Our political programme ran counter to dictatorship in all its forms, whilst correcting certain disorderly aberrations and types of relative anarchy which can easily blight democratic regimes on the European model. We sought to provide the State with fairly strong powers and to put forward a new formula for democracy.

Our success would have liberated the Arabs on another level as well: they would have been freed of their servility and false hopes *vis-a-vis* the U.S. and U.S.S.R. In the end, what is required of us is to be ourselves, to carry out our own collective destiny and not to dress up in weird and incongruous disguises.

Personally, I am a partisan of the 'third force', the 'third way' as I call it, based on a critical approach to progress and evolution, a discriminating synthesis of the two other main tendencies in the world, Sovietism and Americanism, which get copied in so many ways. The position is a difficult one since civilization is nearly always compounded of plagiarisms; as I said before, man is an excellent mimic, and there is a bit of the sheep in all of us. False concepts of industrial and economic progress predominate: an endless irrational plunge into the Gehenna of consumerism. Underlying it all is the cardinal sin of assuming that man has unlimited and innumerable desires which extend beyond the fulfilment of certain natural and properly delimited needs. This new form of dissipation, be it modelled on Pascal or on Lucifer, implies a false notion of human nature and the destinies of the spirit. For us, the aim is to swim against the tide, to escape the prevailing current and reach firm ground. This message, this appeal for a return to rationality, to values, to an economy of men and things in the classical sense, is finding a wider and wider audience today. There are good reasons to have hope. This 'third current', this alternative form of civilization and practice, belongs both to the East, as it reawakens to its cultural heritage, and to Europe, as it regains consciousness of its humanism and its role in the world. It has implications for foreign policy as well as for domestic affairs and everyday life. But most of the Third World nations, including those of the Arab world, have con-tented themselves with a policy of positive neutralism, without really under-standing the implications and the underlying motivations.

Our success in Lebanon — an apparently insignificant event in a tiny country — would in fact have released the long pent-up energies of Arab nationalism. It would have borne within it the germ of the only realistic and rational project for unity, a federative union of Arab peoples, which has little in common with the phoney projects, the wordy slogans and the various underhand manoeuvres advanced under that name by the present half-hearted Arab leaders, caught as they are between the devil and the deep blue sea.

Furthermore, our success in Lebanon would have had immediate reper-cussions on the proposed plan for a solution to the Palestinian problem — a solution which has, until now, been framed in incomplete, ineffective and plainly immoral terms.

Finally, one should not overlook the influence which could have been exercised by a Lebanon which had regained its dynamism and integrity: the movement to liberate the land of Palestine, the contribution to that effort made by oil revenues, and the level of aid granted to the underdeveloped Arab States, to the peoples of the Third World and to Europe itself would all have been stimulated thereby. It is criminal that Arab financial might is not used to further the Arab cause, to promote liberation and to serve the needy nations of the world.

Why did you not make a revolution?

Perhaps that was a political mistake. We felt that it was not in the interests of the country to create too great a separation between the various regions. We had no wish to see Lebanon become a kind of Korea. Our primary aim was to unite Lebanon, we did not want it to break into two regions, two economic regimes. A second reason is that we expected that at any moment the whole business would be over and things would return to normal. But the war dragged on, the Syrians denied us the decisive military victory. They surrounded us. It took the arrival of the Arab troops to conclude an armistice and to calm everybody down. A third reason is that we were too busy with the day-to-day struggle. We needed political support, and we found that it was not forthcoming, neither from the Arab countries, nor from Europe, nor from the United States, and not even from the Soviet Union. The mirage of Geneva prevailed. And we were too tired, too over-extended, too desperate almost, to undertake a successful social and economic upheaval.

How do you see your political future?

I have no idea. Often, events decide for one. But I think I am gradually going to withdraw from politics; for instance, I will soon give up my post as the representative of this district in the Chamber of Deputies. Then I shall move slowly toward retirement and concentrate more on intellectual and spiritual investigations of the problems of finding peace. The ripe fruit must slowly detach itself and then fall to complete the cycle. Everything will come in its own time, spontaneously and without effort: activity in inactivity, inactivity within activity, it is all the same. A mandate as Deputy weighs heavily, especially when one feels that one could have done more to fulfil it. I want to be free, more tranquil, I want to have more time to concentrate on the affairs of the Progressive Socialist Party. I also intend to work towards the publication of certain mystical writings, in Arabic, French and English. And there is an important project which I am not sure I will be able to carry through: to establish a microfilm library of all the manuscripts and books of Gramarye in Arabic which have not yet been published. There must be over two million of them. Dr. Zakkar, Professor at the Arab University of Beirut, set up a similar project; at one stage Libya seemed interested in the idea, and then, I am not sure why, decided not to put up the L£10 million necessary to implement it. The committee will have to go knocking on other doors. I am also interested in certain studies of Arab and Hindu natural medicine, both ancient and modern. We should be able to collaborate with the modern health food magazines which are increasingly numerous in Europe and the United States. A friend of mine, a famous Hindu doctor from Bombay, is thinking of coming to Lebanon to study ancient Arab medicine and contemporary popular practices. One can do a great deal in a single life, whilst appearing to do nothing.

And that is more interesting than being a Lebanese Deputy?

Infinitely more interesting. And sometimes, so is idling about, when you come down to it. The Chinese are right to say that one should learn the art of idleness, how to look at the sky and the sea and the greenery for hours on end. It is a fairly honourable task. After all, as Aristotle said, the purpose of life is pure meditation: 'acting without acting'.

Aristocrats have rarely led a revolution throughout its course. Usually, they set it going and then are replaced halfway through by others who complete it. Did your position allow you to carry a revolution through to its conclusion, especially within the Arab context?

To talk in terms of aristocrats is already to import categories from the West . . . . The distinction rests on notions that degenerate quickly in the hands of ideologues and politicians and leave them holding only a myth. As for me, I do not use these mental categories, I do not feel that I am an aristocrat, I am unaware of the aristocrat you seem to see in me. I am a man and that is all.

The only sense in which I am proud to be an aristocrat is quite different: it involves the aspiration to the best in ourselves, the urge to spread our wings, to ascend and free ourselves. There is an aristocracy of the soul, irrespective of denomination, which gives us all our sense of honour, our reason for working, thinking, loving and living.

Our civilization — truly materialistic in this respect — has degraded all these social notions, every good and beautiful deed, and turned men into the clans and classes of a giant herd. And the ideologues of every ilk have an endless opportunity to conjure up their illusions, be they proletarian, bourgeois or aristocratic.

Obviously, one has to take the existence of classes into account in every society, even socialist, communist or nationalist ones. But these classes are the expression of the various social and economic functions which pertain to all societies. It is because some — not all — Marxist interpretations refuse to go beyond the mental categories of class, and cannot see them as normal functions of that organic being which is society, that their interpretations

119

end up by being incapable of depicting social and economic reality as it truly is. Class is a barrier to realism and objectivity.

In Lebanon, as in France many people think that, having so many enemies, you are almost bound to be the target of an assassination attempt.

It is possible. I have already survived two such attempts, one in 1962, another a little later. And yes, people are talking about the possibility once again.

But you take absolutely no precautions!

A few precautions. But what is due to happen will happen.

And is it not likely that there will be those who feel that the road to a 'peaceful solution' is to physically eliminate all those who oppose such a solution?

To eliminate them politically, certainly . . . physically too, perhaps. Are we going to witness a series of murders? Probably, unless the rejectionists are brought to their knees by political action. A dirty business, is it not? We have been used, tens of thousands of Lebanese have been immolated so that at the end of the day, the C.I.A., Israel and certain Arab states could turn around and say, 'Well, now, at least you Lebanese are out of it.' The essential thing is to settle the Palestinian problem. Improvements in the democratic institutions, the elimination of certain privileges and the abolition of the caste mentality will have to wait!

Moukhtara, Beirut
September 1976-March 1977

Index